INTERNATIONAL SCHOOLS: NAVIGATING LEADERSHIP CULTURE AND CONTEXT

ANN MCPHEE
with
PAM MUNDY

Copyright © 2023 Ann McPhee with Pam Mundy
All rights reserved
First Edition

Fulton Books
Meadville, PA

Published by Fulton Books 2023

ISBN 979-8-88982-432-9 (paperback)
ISBN 979-8-88982-434-3 (digital)

Printed in the United States of America

CHAPTER 1

Let's Go!

Is leadership different in an international context? Oh, yes!

The challenge is deciding what makes leading in a country that is not your home, or most familiar country, different. Why should leadership in Bogota be so different from leadership in Belgium? Is it that the key competences of leadership are different, or are there other factors involved? These are important questions and the key to success.

This book is a simple guide for a complex subject and one that aims help you tread confidently along the path you have chosen to become an outstanding leader wherever your location.

Leadership is a complex mix of a little of this and a little of that, depending on circumstances. Your challenge is to become knowledgeable, confident, while developing your cultural intelligence so that you make the right choices at the right time that fits your circumstances. Plan your journey for personal development with thoughtfulness and care. This journey involves reflection, challenges, and an honest appraisal of the skills you have. There will be some pleasant surprises as you note the skills that you do have and perhaps some uncomfortable realizations as you identify areas that need honing to greater perfection.

Successful leaders strive continuously to be the best they can be and never assume that they have "arrived" and no longer need to work on themselves. Authentic leaders know that they are never finished learning and understand that leadership is a lifetime's work.

There is no specific formula that will catapult you to the highest level of international leadership. There are simply a range of skills, competencies, and behaviors that can, if skillfully applied, significantly enhance your personal and operational effectiveness.

Our intention in writing this book is to recognize the differences between leading in your home country and when you choose to move internationally. Our aim is to give the reader opportunities to consider these differences within their own skills set. To consider what "culturally intelligent" means and recognize its importance to success. We are asking the questions "Do you have the right skill set? What skills do you feel you would like to acquire and why? How will you set about this?"

We have provided real-life examples that either Pam or I have experienced in our international leadership roles and the challenges faced before bringing them to a successful conclusion, including the lessons we learned and continue to learn along the way.

To begin, you can identify your strengths by taking a macro lens to your personal critical pathway, i.e., the journey toward being a successful international leader, your leadership style, your perception of the challenges you may face, and how you think you will address those issues should you face them.

Next, set out the skills you feel you need to acquire to be a successful international leader and why. Understanding your starting point will make it easier for you to reflect as you make your journey. You will be able to consider if those skills you thought important in the beginning were the right ones. What might you disregard on your international journey as you identify ones that appear more pertinent to your situation?

A trickier task is to then identify how you behave and respond under pressure. To do this, you must recognize the behaviors that you are most comfortable with, those habits you have formed over time, for good or ill. How well do you manage confrontational colleagues or challenging parents? How do you feel about speaking in front of large audiences in which many nationalities—possibly many languages and cultures—are represented? The good news is that the journey for improvement can take you as long as you like. The first step is to set out upon it.

Everyone, whether a leader or not, has their own view of leadership skills and effectiveness. It is worth remembering that we are never as good or bad as we *think* we are and never as good or bad as some people *say* we are!

The list of leadership characteristics below is a starting point. This isn't about adding one characteristic per week to your skill set but an incremental approach to each skill or attribute. As you reflect on them, take pride in the ones you recognize as strengths and identify those that offer you opportunities for improvement.

Mindset attributes:
- Honesty
- Humility
- Integrity
- Authenticity
- Curiosity

Interpersonal skills:
- Excellent communication
- Valuing people
- Listening
- Motivational
- Encouraging

Proactive skills:
- Creativity
- Tenacity
- High standards
- Courage
- Decisiveness

Keep this list handy as a baseline checklist. Ask a few professional and genuinely critical friends if they agree about which traits you believe you possess. This may generate a conversation around how you and your leadership style are perceived. Be ready—this will be the start of your in-depth self-analysis.

A real-life example

In 2012, Harvard Business School Professor Anita Elberse examined the leadership style of former Manchester United Football Club Manager Sir Alex Ferguson and built around it a case study that was published in the Harvard Review in October 2013.

Whether or not you are a fan of the team or of the man, there is no denying Sir Alex's skill in building successful teams while managing the vagaries of international communities with their diverse beliefs and cultural backgrounds and all the while under scrutiny from the world's media.

Professor Elberse discussed eight leadership lessons that captured the crucial elements of Ferguson's leadership approach. These were as follows:

1. Start with the foundations of the team as it currently exists.
2. "Dare greatly" to build and mold your team.
3. Set high standards, share them explicitly, and hold everyone to them.
4. Never ever cede control.
5. Match the message to the moment.
6. Prepare to win.
7. Rely on the power of observation.
8. Never stop adapting.

Now revisit the list of your own leadership characteristics again in light of Sir Alex's lessons. Which of them resonate with you? How good are you, for example, at matching the message to the moment?

The Harvard Business Review case study also noted that, generally, disgruntled teams often refer to their senior leaders as "the Management" while contented teams talk about "the Leadership." Interesting!

Forensic and robust analysis of your characteristics, approaches, attitudes, and styles will help you know yourself better. The experience of integration into a new international setting may also help you discover which aspects you want to replicate. In this way, you can get clear on which characteristics and skills you want to develop and which attitudes you want to remove from your personal style.

In this book, we have added, at the end of each chapter, something entitled "The power of 3": three quotes and three books for further reading should you be interested in exploring the issues raised further. The quotes will provide motivation, encouragement, or a pause for reflection. They may trigger something within you that empowers you to move on. The power of 3 is there for the reader to make of these books and quotes as they wish. They can help you reflect on your learning or propel you into a specific skill's area that interests you. We hope they prove both memorable and useful because three things are easy to remember!

The power of 3

Three quotations to help you reflect or inspire you:

> Self-awareness is where effective leadership begins. (Lolly Daskin, *Lead from Within*, leadership development)

> Even when personal feedback is presented to us, we're not always open to it, because honest feedback isn't always flattering. Consequently, many of us have a pretty low level of self-awareness. That's unfortunate because self-awareness is an essential first step toward maximising management skills. Self-awareness can improve our judgment and help us identify opportunities for professional development and personal growth. (Raj Soin, *College of Business, Wright State University*)

Self-awareness has too often been relegated to "back-seat" status. A soft skill that's nice-to-have, yet not critical to tangible business performance.

Self-awareness is the most crucial developmental breakthrough for accelerating personal leadership growth and authenticity. Learning to pause to build self-awareness is an evolving process critical to leader success. It is extremely valuable to know ourselves in order to leverage our potentialities. (Kevin Cashman, *Return of Self-Awareness: Research Validates the Bottom Line of Leadership Development*, in Forbes, March 2014)

Three books to challenge your thinking further:

- Collins, James C., and Morten T. Hansen. *Great by Choice: Uncertainty, Chaos, and Luck—Why Some Thrive Despite Them All.* New York, 2011.
- Gallagher, Daniel, and Joseph Costal. *The Self-Aware Leader: A Proven Model for Reinventing Yourself.* Alexandria, Virginia, 2012.
- Alison, Emily, and Laurence Alison. *Rapport: The Four Ways to Read People.* Edbury Digital, July 2020.

CHAPTER 2

Am I Good Enough?

It is not easy to identify your personal leadership style, even in your home country. It is a complex process driven by a personal desire to know when you are demonstrating good leadership and all the while comparing yourself to what you think a great leader should be. This can take a little time to separate!

Many aspiring leaders wrestle daily with the challenge of separating the unrealistic ideal of the supereffective leader from what can really be achieved. Deciding what skills, knowledge, expertise, and courage you will need, and in what quantities, can seem a complex task. It is worth remembering that courage isn't always about standing up and defending a situation loudly but just about getting up the next day and trying again. In this chapter, we are looking at the skills a successful international leader needs to acquire

Climbing Everest

If you are approaching the development of your leadership skills and behaviors with honesty, it may feel like a tough test because you must trust yourself. What are the strengths you have, and what are your opportunities for development? When leaders embark on building their knowledge, they are often amazed at the skills they already have. Self-improvement is like climbing a mountain because the top never seems to get any closer, yet if you climb steadily and purposefully, you will gain altitude with every improvement.

When the challenge of learning how to lead is compounded with a transition to an international context, there is an additional set of challenges to face. Such a move can be stressful or exciting, engendering the fear of failure or the anticipation of success. Either way, the job in hand is to develop a personal leadership style that achieves results wherever you are in the world and whatever team you are leading. At this stage, it is critical not to gloss over the characteristics you already have but identify and acknowledge them, understanding that you can build on them too as you learn and grow.

You may find that some of your characteristics will develop as a natural consequence of your leadership responsibility. Confidence, for example, usually grows with time in a role as we discover what we *can* do. Other characteristics may need more deliberate and systematic development, for example, the ability to have difficult conversations with staff or parents.

It is usually best to manage your self-reflection calmly, i.e., choose a time where you can have peace, enabling good concentration while working through the leadership actions that you have identified you feel need to be worked on. There are books, podcasts, articles, and webinars galore that offer advice about what a leader should be, do, have, and even how a leader should dress for success.

Should you be smarter? Stronger? More caring? Less caring? More direct? Less direct? Should you lead by empowering people? Distributing leadership? Leading from behind? Leading from the front?

The list extends daily as new research on leadership is validated. If you read some of these during your day, you could become overwhelmed and feel there isn't anything you are good at which is, of course, not the case.

It is worth taking some substantial time to identify the specific characteristics that great leaders demonstrate, especially those with an internationally proven track record. Start with yourself because *you* are the most important person on this journey of self-discovery and professional growth.

The American writer Ralph Marston is quoted as saying: "Success in any endeavour depends on the degree to which it is an expression of your true self."

What you are trying to achieve is a leadership style that is wholly yours, that you can wear with confidence and humility. A style that is respectful and brings successful outcomes for both team members and you, the international team leader.

Vision or nightmare

People who are impact-oriented have a clear vision: a crystallized picture in their minds of where they want to go and why. What makes them leaders, however, is their ability to inspire others by sharing the vision through great communication. (The importance of communication will be covered several times throughout the book as without it, all other leadership skills will not be as successful.) Inspiring people to buy into the vision and see the opportunities that it presents for them by taking part in its development is an *essential* leadership skill to acquire.

"Vision without action is a daydream. Action without vision is a nightmare."

This Japanese proverb is one for all leaders to live by. It reminds us not to rush in before we are clear about the journey we want to go on and have inspired the team come along with us.

In an international setting, the colleagues we need to bring with us often come with a rich tapestry of diverse backgrounds, experiences, working cultures, and attitudes. For this reason, the international arena adds an additional layer of challenge to the task of sharing your vision in a meaningful way. A good first step is to ensure that colleagues understand both the purpose of the vision and exactly what will be achieved.

Leadership today is much more about authentic collaboration and collegiate working, otherwise known as systemic leadership, than an autocratic "follow me" style. The traditional employee attitude of *Tell me* has shifted to *Ask me*, and that has caused leaders to change from *You will* to *Shall we*. How effectively your vision is communicated in a culturally appropriate way is critical to your success. A by-product of this, and one that a team leader needs to achieve, is great buy-in from all colleagues regardless of cultural background.

Transience

In many international organizations, they are often staffed by a transient workforce with short renewable contracts being the norm. This means that leaders of these organizations must harness the hearts and minds of people quickly and gain their support to effectively transfer their vision into practical reality. They will also need to repeat this process frequently as staff change. It should never be assumed that once shared and acted upon, your vision will continue to guide and motivate without regular repetition and revision.

Engagement

Lee Cockerell, in his book *Creating Magic*[1], describes his role as the operations officer of Disney. Every day he reminded himself that the team was not comprised of his *employees* but his *people* and that fostering participation and engagement at all levels resulted in high morale, authentic commitment, and real results.

Most of us can recall meetings at which we listened to a leader tell us what was to be done by when, and we leave the meeting with a set of tasks set. Team members leave such meetings with little sense of real commitment to the purpose or outcome. Indeed, many have never had the big picture vision explained at any time and have only been required to be receivers, ready to complete their allotted tasks in a vacuum and arrive at the next meeting for the next download.

However, when a vision is shared regularly with team members and reshaped by being viewed through a collective lens, improvements in motivation are swift. When people's views and ideas are sought, meeting rooms become the engine room of success and productivity.

---

[1] Lee Cockerell, *Creating Magic* (Publisher: Currency, October 2008).

In an international setting where a high proportion of support staff may be locally hired, specific attention must be paid to their inclusion. Asking a colleague who speaks the home language proficiently to brief the team in their mother tongue is often more effective than providing a printed briefing, even if it has been translated.

When we focus on being both visionary and consultative, it helps us remember the importance of other voices in our decision-making. We need to share our intended outcomes regularly with our team and make time to both listen to them as well as, hopefully, motivate them through discussion of the vision, e.g., "How will *we* make this happen?"

This is a *necessary* skill to acquire—this balance between listening to views and making improvements while achieving the target the leader has in mind. Do not rush. Team members must also be helped to understand that not all suggestions will be acted upon. Even though every member of a team has an equal voice, the leader is responsible for the team's outcomes. How tactfully this relationship is managed can make the difference between success or failure.

Whichever way you do it, taking time to explain your vision in a respectful and culturally appropriate way as well as include your team in its development will reap many benefits, the major one being buy-in.

International intelligence

We could call the ability to identify the best way to share information in the cultural context in which you are operating "international (or cultural) intelligence." Internationally intelligent leaders always take time to identify all the languages that are spoken, for example, as well as how proficient people may be in reading and writing in their home language and in English. With their team, they plan carefully how information will be shared to ensure full involvement, demonstrating that all staff are valued.

Internationally intelligent leaders never make assumptions. As the adage reminds us, "Never assume because it makes an ass out of you and me." Internationally minded leaders also ensure that what is agreed, or planned for, takes into account cultural customs, e.g., no meetings either in person or virtually on Friday in the Middle East as this is a holy day in the Islamic calendar.

Being genuine

When each team member knows their role in the bigger picture and understands fully the part they must play, then a sense of motivation and pride will prevail. Communicating pleasure and pride in an individual's or team's achievement as progress is made on a project is another habit well worth cultivating. Everyone needs to feel appreciated. Choosing the right moment to show sincere appreciation, for a valid reason, will pay handsomely. Praise for praise's sake, or praise that is given just to be seen to be recognizing effort because you know you should, is picked up on by employees very quickly. Be genuine in your appreciation.

Achieving a strong and genuine sense of teamwork is particularly significant in international leadership success. Blending different ways of working, and sometimes values, to ensure that the people within your team have the skills, knowledge, and appreciation of the task is time consuming but sets the team up to succeed. It shows them daily that their commitment is both witnessed and appreciated. It is more than a worthwhile strategy. It shows genuine respect and demonstrates a valuing of a colleague's contribution. They can share their sense of achievement within the team. They are working *with* you to achieve the vision.

Integrity and honesty

For obvious reasons, there is almost always a strong expectation that leaders should have integrity and should be honest. We all want to be led by people whose actions match their words and whose words reflect the truth. Arguably, this kind of authenticity should be easy to achieve because no special knowledge, training, or experience is required to have integrity and be honest; they are simple moral choices.

The expectation that all leaders should have these traits is so universal that it would be hard to find a leader who doesn't claim to be honest and have integrity. However, judging by the number of dysfunctional schools and organizations that have management problems stemming from issues of honesty and/or lack of integrity, keeping our word and speaking the truth is neither universal nor easy.

Positions of responsibility are often fraught with situations in which the best moral choice is not always clear or easy, especially in the heat of the moment. Consider the leader who feels overwhelmed by targets but doesn't want to question them for fear of appearing weak. The temptation can be very strong to simply accept overambitious goals and run the risk of overpromising and under delivering. The resulting pressure that this can place on a team is a recipe for stress, conflict, underperformance, and the impression that the team has been set up to fail. The leader who tried hard not to let down the organization has ended up letting down the team.

For the leader who inherits a team that has experienced a situation such as this, it is important to recognize and quickly correct such a cultural legacy. The more authentic leaders are, the more colleagues and peers will learn to trust them. Our behavior needs to be the same whether we are looking up, or down, the hierarchy of our organization. To promise our boss that it is possible to deliver something that we clearly cannot merely delays the inevitable discovery of the fact later.

Reputation

The world of international leadership is very small, and reputations form quickly with the aid of social media. For this reason, it is wise to remember that a team's collective perceptions about how they have been led can have a wide and long-lasting impact on peers' opinions of us. If a team feels that their reputations have been sacrificed to their leader's ego, this perception can become a communicated reality very quickly. Reputational hangovers can take a very long time to fix and, in some cases, never.

It is undoubtedly a serious challenge to remain authentic 24-7 no matter how great a leader you are. Leaders are human after all.

In the book, *The Authentic Leader: It's about Presence, Not Position*,[2] authors David Irvine and Jim Reger researched the leadership behaviors of forty-five leaders perceived to be authentic. They drew out the impact an authentic presence has on individuals and teams. The impact of this one behavior outweighs many of the others. It not only establishes a personal leadership ethic, but it also demonstrates strength of character in believing truth and honesty are paramount in successful leadership.

Gossip

There is some truth in the popular saying, "Gossip is when you hear something that you like about someone that you don't." It is easy to get caught up in casual conversations in which information is disclosed inappropriately. Sharing idle talk or rumors about people can seem like harmless fun at the time, but it should be avoided because unguarded moments can be years in repair.

If you do find yourself in the unfortunate position of being confronted by a colleague about something they have heard you say about them, your response will involve a careful choice. What would you do? Would you hotly deny it, or would you own up and apologize? Being authentic at times like these is very hard. Feelings of shame and fear can blind us to the consequences of denial and the opportunity to strengthen the relationship through honesty. If whip-smart, developing leaders learn from challenging moral dilemmas and make sure they never make the same mistake twice.

The international context may also be a factor to consider because in some countries, gossip is almost part of the cultural norm. If that's the case, then a leader would do well to counsel their team to be even more careful than usual about what they share. That is being internationally intelligent and doing your leadership homework. Knowing the country and the expectation and practices of its people is time very well spent.

---

[2] David Irvine and Jim Reger, *The Authentic Leader: It's about Presence, Not Position* (Publisher: DC Press, July 2006).

It is also smart to know the saying, "*We don't do that in XXXX (insert your own organization)!*" will *not* help resolve a situation, just demonstrate a leader's absolute lack of cultural intelligence. Conflict situations are rarely resolved with a quick fix, so in most cases, it is best to take time to reflect on the best course of action, rather than rushing in on the spur of the moment, especially when emotions are still running high. Try to think beyond the interpersonal level and look at things from an organizational perspective. What are the implications of what has happened, and what impact would action, or inaction, have and on whom? In an international setting, it is also critical to consider what possible cultural and political consequences there may be. In most simple circumstances, the implications are minimal, but never take it for granted. Do not rush to judgment or launch in without being sure of the best course of action.

On the flip side, make sure you don't take too long in your deliberations because a perceived lack of action on your part can be misconstrued as an unwillingness to deal with it or a lack of concern. The unavoidable fact is that you must address the issue no matter how awkward, uncomfortable, or confrontational it may turn out to be. Effective leaders do not enjoy such situations, no one does; they simply understand that it must be handled and that it is their responsibility to do so.

It is on occasions such as these that leaders are most conspicuous because the rest of the team look to them to intervene. A team's assessment of their leader is likely to be significantly affected by how they respond to such situations. Once again, integrity is expected and must be demonstrated, sometimes even overtly. When integrity is partnered with courage, it enhances the working environment for everyone. It shows respect and models the behaviors that are expected from every member of the team.

Integrity comes into play not just in what you do but how you do it. Make it a specific rule never to tackle difficult people's conversations publicly however irritated or exasperated you may be feeling. There is nothing to be gained other than personal embarrassment by putting someone down in public. This will damage your reputation beyond repair and change the working atmosphere of your team.

Your colleagues will be cautious and more reserved with you, anxious to ensure they are not dealt with in a similar way themselves. This adversely affects the pace of change and the development of the culture you are trying to achieve. Don't do it.

A real-life example

In a supermarket recently, a colleague of ours was having some groceries packed by a very pleasant young man. During the transaction, the young man's supervisor approached and remonstrated with him loudly for a minor infraction of rules in front of a queue of people at the till. It was clear that several people in the queue became uncomfortable and felt embarrassed by the supervisor's aggressive behavior, which demonstrated an obvious disrespect for his employee and an immature attitude toward leadership. Furthermore, the supervisor did not seem able to see the discomfort experienced by his colleagues or his customers. He appeared to be showing off his power, perhaps thinking this is what leaders do to improve performance.

Our colleague waited until the supervisor walked away from the till and followed him, asking politely if they may have a word in private. She explained how, as a customer, she did not like being made to feel embarrassed and suggested that he might want to reflect on how he should have dealt with this issue. They spoke for over ten minutes, and the supervisor explained that his own experience of being supervised was of being regularly "told off," and yet on reflection, he could remember that he didn't like being addressed in this manner himself.

One may hope that following the experience, this young supervisor might act differently in future. He may even go on to learn more about employee engagement and people-centered leadership. Interestingly, the exchange also made our colleague reflect on her own approach. She was proud to have found the courage to stand up for the grocery packer and felt that she had intervened with integrity while not belittling anyone, either personally or in public. It certainly would have been much easier for her to walk away, muttering under her breath and feeling disgruntled for the whole day!

Listening carefully

Dealing with a very public issue in an international organization requires time for both sets of people to share their side of events. Leaders need to be listeners because there are always two sides to every story. It is also important to have a heightened awareness of the cultural norms that can add important contextual information regarding the issue, which may have been heightened by such influences.

In the final analysis, it must be clear as to what was and was not acceptable and what behavior is expected going forward. There may need to be a private apology to an individual or an apology to a team. Apologizing in some cultures is viewed as losing face, and so once again, international intelligence is key to finding the right way through.

If colleagues are not able to comply with expectations or the situation is more severe, then a leader may need to be resolute and tough in decision-making. It is essential to always be courteous and fair because no matter how angry or unreasonable someone is or how inappropriate their behavior, the manner with which they are dealt with will always air in the public arena. How many times have we heard colleagues say, "Well, I didn't agree with that, but at least I was allowed to have my say" or "At least they were fair"?

Respecting others and being judged as an internationally minded and fair person with demonstrable integrity and courage are great attributes to have and have recognized. There are no shortcuts to achieving this. They must be earned. If this is how you are perceived, then you are beginning to build trust within your team. Acting appropriately, respectfully, and fairly are game changers.

Fair or unfair? That is the question

The same challenge applies when a leader is perceived by the team to be subjected to unfair and inappropriate treatment themselves. A common concern is, "If I complain, will I be penalized in some way?" Some leaders actively cultivate such an approach.

This is another occasion when digging deep for courage is necessary because there can be uncertainty about the outcome. Providing people with a safe environment, where they feel able to air their concerns without fear of retribution, is a great place to end up. This is, however, not at all easy to achieve as people worry about what they are told and the reality. Will it really be safe?

It is reasonable for a leader also to hope that this is the environment in which they themselves operate, either because they have a supportive human resource directorate (talent management) or senior leaders who believe in and practice open, honest, and respectful discussions.

Confidentiality

A major issue that requires serious consideration and planning for is when a colleague says, "I want this to remain confidential." Leaders should be cautious in this situation because one simply cannot promise confidentiality before hearing what is about to be disclosed. If this happens to you, it is imperative to stop the conversation immediately and explain that it may not be possible to promise confidentiality because of safeguarding reasons, operational priorities, commercial sensitivity, or any number of other concerns connected with the responsibility that a leader carries. Explaining in this way gives the other person a choice about whether to continue or not. The very last thing good leaders wish to do is betray a confidence, but the nature of the information shared may mean that it *must* be passed on and sometimes without the person knowing. This kind of disclosure, if the person is not prepared for it to happen, can harm a team and a leader's ability to build trust and mutual respect.

Communication

Good leaders are good communicators. They *hear* what is being said and *listen* to both the explicit content and the implied message. They:

- Are clear
- Speak succinctly
- Get to the point

- Know the power of silence
- Know the leverage of reflective responses
- Encourage input
- Share appropriate information in a timely manner
- Reward the success openly and willingly
- Manage the mistakes of others sensitively
- Can say, "I got it wrong"
- Manage conflict successfully and without drama
- Manage change smoothly
- Are courageous

One of the most useful questions leaders can ask is "How?" Another is "I wonder…" Both are highly effective at provoking a better suggestion from a colleague without directly asking for one.

In her book, *Conversational Intelligence*[3], Judith E. Glaser talks about a conversational dashboard.

Level 1: "Transactional": Best described as *Tell and Ask*. There is limited trust.

Level 2: "Positional": Best described as *Advocate and Inquire*. "I am advocating for what I want, inquiring about your beliefs, so I can influence you to *my* point of view."

Level 3: "Transformational": Best described as *Share and Discover*. "I will open up my inner thoughts, ideas, and feelings to you." Others receive the signal that you are willing to be influenced, you care about them, and that they can trust you to experiment and innovate with them.

Transformational conversations are clearly the ones to work toward and practice daily to develop this strategy. It isn't easy to do and does need practice.

---

[3] Judith E. Glaser, *Conversational Intelligence* (Publisher: Bibliomotion Inc., 2014).

Real-life example

In the very early days as a school's adviser in England, a colleague met with a head of school and the senior leadership team who were facing a very difficult time driven by the local authority, a regional governing body for schools in the UK. The challenge was to improve their high-end exam outcomes for students aged sixteen years to eighteen years. The school's adviser started the meeting by revisiting the aspects of the senior leadership team's current practice that had been largely unsuccessful, and at that point, an immediate change in atmosphere was felt in the room. The body language changed from openness to heads down and shoulders hunched.

The adviser knew instantly that a serious error had been made in the approach. The purpose that day had been to discuss how the senior leadership team would work *together* to bring about the improvement necessary to transform the leadership and improve exam outcomes. The adviser recognized the approach had had the opposite effect and so apologized immediately and changed track. However, the damage was done. It took many weeks longer to build trust and confidence than if the adviser had started instead with a more open process of sharing and discovery. Perception, on both sides, becomes reality without the essential clarity.

Characteristics of successful leaders are often in the eye of the beholder. The ones that we have discussed in detail in this chapter are ones that appear on many lists. These are ones that are deeply personal to a leader and should be added into the nonnegotiable mix. This is not a mix-and-match list or a choose-what-you-feel-you-need-to-do-better list. This should provide a real challenging time for honest reflection. Are you all of these? If not, then what are you going to do about it?

1) *Humility*: There's nothing worse than a leader telling everyone, continuously, how great they are.
2) *Agility*: To move forward honestly in the face of obstacles
3) *Reflection*: Make time to reflect on self and the actions taken, genuinely celebrating what the team did well.

4) *Genuineness*: A clearly demonstrated desire to help others grow without self-gratifying intent
5) *Appropriate sense of humor*: This is a very tricky one and a cultural minefield. It is reliant on a team knowing itself and the international mix of people on the team. One to work out perhaps during a transformational conversation!

While reviewing these characteristics, you may have reflected on your own experiences with a leader you have either admired or not. One thing is clear, you cannot be an effective leader unless you know what effective leadership characteristics are. This is at both a deeply personal level and an operational level. Work to understand why they make such a positive impact on people and self-reflect honestly on where you feel you are on your journey to high-quality leadership.

It is exciting to begin thinking about style and characteristics and how they fit together to create the blueprint for the leader you want to be.

The power of 3

Three quotations to ponder on:

> Transformation is a process, and as life happens there are tons of ups and downs. It's a journey of discovery—there are moments on mountaintops and moments in deep valleys of despair. (Rick Warren, American writer)

> None of us is as smart as all of us. (Ken Blanchard, keynote speaker, author, and business guru specializing in leadership development, management, and training)

> Good thinkers are always in demand. A person who knows how, may always have a job, but the person who knows why, will always be

his boss. (*How Successful People Think,* John C. Maxwell [Publisher: Center Street, 2009])

Three books to challenge your thinking further:

- Marquet, L. David. *Turn the Ship Around.* New York, 2013.
- Marciano, Paul L. *Carrots and Sticks Don't Work: Build a Culture of Employee Engagement with the Principles of RESPECT.* New York, 2010.
- Haudan, Jim. *The Art of Engagement: Building the Gap Between People and Possibility.* Sylvania, Ohio, 2017.

CHAPTER 3

It Feels a Little Strange

Now down to business. It's time to go deeper in a process of self-analysis, comparing your own leadership style and behaviors with those exhibited by outstanding international leaders. This will give you the opportunity to focus fully on confirming what you are doing well and crucially confirm if what you identified earlier as attributes and skills to enhance or acquire are accurate.

In Chapter 2, we looked at key characteristics of great leaders. Before you began reading this book, you might also have begun to identify the key features of your own style of leadership. We will now look forensically at the key skills and processes of effective leaders and assess more formally the extent to which you are successfully acquiring and applying them.

To become a leader with a holistic approach to both managing yourself and leading others means taking a leadership stance, i.e., as the leader, can I share my expectations well? This means are you clear about how you will represent yourself, your values, expectations, and decisions.

Readiness to embrace change

Leaders, both actual and aspiring, strive to develop and improve their leadership style and skills as they know nothing remains static.

They need to be ready to cope with the rapid pace of change that every organization faces today in a shrinking global work environment.

Working with international colleagues often involves online meetings, interviews, and connections. As a result of the Fourth Industrial Revolution[4], much of our communication is now conducted in a hybrid mode—partly in person, partly with a virtual element. The pace of change is challenging for leaders as these are relatively unchartered waters. A leader must manage the complexity of these changes in a way that demonstrates clear and unambiguous communication alongside a calm "we can manage this" manner. This will ensure a coherent process with effective outcomes. All too often there is no time to practice and perfect a new leadership skill before its circumstances mean that it must be used. The pressure and pace of work means that we are constantly learning on the job.

Rather than getting overwhelmed, be true to your own management and leadership style. Your preference may be a calm decisive approach with colleagues, which enables steady progress and success. If it isn't your go-to style, there may be times when the pace of change requires it. Be very conscious of when this is.

Ram Charan, one of the world's preeminent advisers to CEOs and boards (including GE, Bank of America, Verizon, and the Royal Bank of Scotland Group), points out in his interview with the Harvard Business Review's Senior Editor Melinda Merino in 2013 that:

> The rapid pace of change *is* the most difficult aspect for leaders to come to terms with. Decisions leaders make will be judged in the court of public opinion and in the "anti-social media" world of Facebook, Twitter, blogs et al and no one will know for certain if you are beginning, developing or mastering a new leadership skill and "trying it out." You are devoid of time to practice!

---

[4] Nicholas Davis and Klaus Schwab, *Shaping the Future of the Fourth Industrial Revolution* (Currency, 2018).

There is no place for leaders to hide; there is no time for them to learn everything they would ideally like to know. There is little opportunity to build a strategy, let alone reflect on it. Leaders must deliver, often under significant pressure, and bring projects to fruition. At an international level, leaders need the additional skill of being able to understand the cultural context of their businesses and projects, developing an awareness of subtle nuances within the local and national community that matter to the people they work with.

In the case of international and future-oriented leadership, we must be clear about how and when we may need to modify our leadership style to reflect the local culture. What skills from our professional toolbox are most applicable? Making a well-judged start is important, but we can also expect the skills and strategies required of us to change over time as we mature and develop. Leaders should always be alert to possible changes and be sure to have constructive conversations with the leadership team beforehand to discuss benefits and drawbacks should these changes come to fruition.

Effective decision-making

The essence of leadership is knowing how to make decisions, garner agreement, and most importantly, communicate the decision clearly, including the processes that led to it. In chapter 2, we discussed the importance of honest communications conveyed clearly without the use of jargon. Effective communication of strategy by these means will ensure that decisions lead to actions and ultimately the desired result.

Good leaders usually have people they can depend on when there are times of pressure. These are people with whom they can discuss the proposed and revised strategy or resolution with alacrity and confidentiality. If other team members can see how time, no matter how swift, is taken to ensure the right decision or response is made and the decision and the rationale clearly shared, then it is likely the team will be supportive. Good teams want their leader to succeed and offer support willingly when communication is excellent.

Selecting modes and channels of communication

In international settings, it is important to apprise yourself of how well the local contractors, employees, or stakeholders understand English (or the language in which you will be conducting your business). Early on, you will need to decide whether interpreters will be necessary and whether some other forms of communication, such as printed briefings, may be appropriate for transmitting certain information. *Consider your choices carefully.* If using an interpreter, they need to critically be a good linguist and someone with emotional intelligence and tact. You may find that a combination of communication channels, both oral and written, work best. Determine when confidentiality is needed and therefore which is the most secure method. Social media platforms and applications also present possibilities for public engagement. Choose wisely! For weekly updates, a short video could be preferable to a lengthy newsletter.

Community sensitivity

In an international institution, it is very rare indeed to find that everyone has the same level of English language use and comprehension, so the decision about how to communicate, perhaps your first as a leader, is one that you must be sure to get right. Understanding the community in terms of both cultural context and local needs will go a long way toward demonstrating respect for colleagues and stakeholders and a determination to be an inclusive leader.

Identify one or more individuals who, within the team, can best guide you to the most effective approaches. Check out any suggestions with your team and then put them to use perhaps using a mixture of methods.

For example, parent meetings where the first language is Spanish and the teaching is in English may benefit from a meeting where a presentation plays in Spanish at the same time as the leader is sharing information in English.

There is also the strategy of using a school simultaneous interpreter with individual parent headsets.

Preparing new staff for their cultural shift by presenting to them in their home country (UK if there is a large number coming for the start of the summer term). The presentation is about culture, the school, and community expectations, including local courtesies and customs.

Communicating well however difficult the information

Sharing your vision and that of your organization will be a key goal. At the same time, listening to staff and community and valuing people and their contributions are so very important. Effective communication strategies will enable you to do all these things. However, achieving this is not always easy.

Clarity of messaging helps the team understand your intentions and realize that you recognize and accept their needs. Showing this deep understanding will open the door for you to participate in the growth and development of the team and the institution.

However, there always comes a time when a leader must make a potentially unpopular decision and implement its outcomes. No matter how skilled that person is, making such decisions is hard and certainly unwelcome; it may even feel impossible knowing, as you do, that the ripples may last for some time and that you will have to field the consequences.

How you deal with making difficult decisions is a complex matter, and the best solution may change with maturity. As an early career leader, you may find that your approach differs from that of a person with many years' experience. For example, as a relatively new leader, you may find that your high level of anxiety leads you to a softer, more persuasive style hoping that this will work better (it very rarely does), while a leader with many years of experience may have the approach that resonates with more confidence, is direct, and a swifter conclusion reached.

Collaboration but not at all costs

A collaborative style of decision-making enables your team to participate, contribute, and have a sense of ownership of the project;

however, many leaders attempting to use this approach overlook the need for regular revision against progress targets. Garnering opinions and ideas are valuable, but if after an extended period of discussion and collaboration, the team is unsure how to proceed, a successful outcome may become compromised. It falls to the leader to draw the threads together, review regularly but make the final decision. So be ready to notice when the team starts to flounder. That will be your cue to step in and take things forward.

Sharing unwelcome news

How different nationalities and cultures receive unpleasant messages is significant. No matter how skillful an orator, how emotionally intelligent and astute the approach, or how well attuned the "gut" instinct is, there can potentially be times when sharing unwelcome news is truly unpleasant and elicits adverse reactions.

If you have difficult news to impart, reflect carefully in advance to ensure the message is delivered at an appropriate time and place, in the most effective and respectful way. Plan ahead and don't wait until the "have to" moment. Discuss fully with relevant colleagues how best to manage the communication and agree on the most effective method and approach. Less palatable news delivered efficiently is far better than a long lead-in.

It is incumbent on the leaders to make good decisions about time, setting, and mode of communication then deliver the message clearly and directly in a manner that is clear and respectful. There may be times when your listeners are given the opportunity to ask questions, but there will also be times when it is not appropriate. Judge wisely.

To deliver a message of this kind within an international setting amongst a culturally diverse staff requires even greater cultural sensitivity than usual. An ill-considered approach may inadvertently cause offense and could result in the focus being diverted away from an effective resolution, and a great many metaphorical bridges will need to be built to reestablish trust.

Where possible, approach difficult situations from a position of collaboration and never with an attitude of aggression. That said, if the time for collaboration is past and a difficult decision must be made, you will need to combine clarity of communication with great contextual and cultural sensitivity in conveying it. Keep your emotional antennae finely tuned using the guidance of trusted local advisers, and you will be able to ensure that the message is effectively communicated, fully understood, and as well received as possible. This should enable you to bring about the required change without confusion or resistance from those affected.

Forward-thinking skills

To drive their institutions forward successfully, leaders are always ready to spot new initiatives and ideas on the horizon, as well as being fully aware of the skills already extant within the team. Good leaders are continually monitoring the skill set in the team to ensure it remains fit for purpose. These are complex processes. If the result is a team in which each staff member has a role matched to their skills, abilities, and attributes, then a very big piece of the leadership puzzle is already in place. It also helps team members to experience their strengths being recognized and any development of a new skill identified and planned for. They are continuing to grow and helping the institution to develop further and feeling valued. If a staff member does not have the skill but does have the potential, effective leaders look at ways to provide relevant professional development opportunities for that person as then everyone benefits.

*Leadership in children's early years'
education is a little different too*

Learning for very young children (early years, kindergarten) has become a focus across many countries and continents in the first quarter of the twenty-first century. Early learning for children as young as two years of age is challenging governments, schools, and providers. When planning for this, we may find ourselves asking the questions:

- What is the cultural approach to early learning in the community/country?
- What do we know, and what do we *think* we know?
- What do we *have* to know?
- What should we *do*, and how should we do it?

These are not questions with simple answers, more so in an international setting, where in addition, we might ask:

- Firstly, the school needs to decide what early learning curriculum or format it is going to follow.
- The team leader then needs to check the skills and approaches the people identified to work in this specialized area have.
- A training program for adults may need to be set up and delivered before working with such young people begins.
- How to communicate with parents is next. Play is a young person's way of working, so if this is a challenge culturally, workshops may be needed with interpreters able to help the community understand the benefits and how they will know what progress is being made.

Parenting

Leaders vary in their beliefs as to what makes great parenting, owing to variation in their own cultural background, childhood experiences, and general expectations of schools. The effective leader draws on positive insights from his or her own experience, whether this be greater sensitivity to problems or situations or an awareness of certain effective measures or techniques that can be applied. However, there will be situations where personal experience is wholly inadequate, and here again, listening and collaboration skills combined with highly attuned cultural antennae will enable the leader to be as adaptable as necessary. It is also necessary to understand acceptable parenting methods in the country you are working in. For some, physical punishment is acceptable for parents to children, so the leader must be aware as they plan their relationship with a parent community.

A key question that the international leader in education will need to ask is How do we select the core national languages into which our documents are translated? There may also be more than one main language in the school as there may be two or three strong communities within the school.

This necessitates an even higher order of international mindedness and also broaches the need for equality. Literal translation may not always result in an accurate meaning being conveyed, owing to loss of nuance and metaphor.

Secondly, in some international contexts, a native speaker may deliver communications more effectively orally as opposed to in a written translation, in which case it is important to check for understanding of the key messages by means of conversation, perhaps in question-and-answer format. Such conversations may then be summarized and translated as a record to be retained and to inform any printed material.

Talking to each other in an international setting

If messages are being delivered through a virtual (digital) route, then it is doubly important to ensure that they are framed in a way that recognizes the language skills of the intended audience. We want people to relate to our message, feel involved, and be keen to participate in the plan we have. Careful preparation will be needed to ensure clear messaging where bilingual support may be necessary.

It is important for international school leaders to inform themselves about changes in the world of international education that may affect their work alongside managing day-to-day changes. Outstanding leaders do *not* rush in with a reaction to anything new. Rather, they take the opportunity to review new ideas and technical innovations, consider their probable impact, and assess their anticipated benefits then calmly discuss all these aspects with relevant colleagues and community members to establish the relevance for the school. This approach determines whether prompt action is needed or whether a wait-and-see model is preferable.

Sharply focused and carefully scheduled strategic planning promotes confidence and a can-do attitude among staff. It can also ensure that parents feel they are well-informed and genuinely valued as authentic partners in their school community. Decisions for the well-being of the school and its students are usually best made based on discussion, consultation, and informed debate.

Valuing consultation in an international setting

International leaders encourage staff to ask and answer questions to ensure the right changes are taking place to ensure either student or school progress. They might include:

- Why is this change necessary?
- How does this change fit within the culture and context of the institution?
- Will staff be responsible for managing parts of the change program?
- What will we do if some staff think the change is good but are not able to manage it with the skills they have now? Have we planned for training?
- What will happen if there is disagreement and dissention? What will our first steps be to help change this view?
- How will successful change be celebrated?

All these questions will quickly arise in an effective leader's mind. Agile leaders are aware that clear, well thought-out responses are the key to successful change management. For leaders in an international educational context, there are additional challenges. Understanding how your community might respond to a particular change is key to determining how you will make and communicate decisions. This will also affect how you plan your delivery of the project. Sensitivity blended with decisiveness is essential to success.

Leaders in an international setting must always use their awareness of the climate and culture of the community in which they work as their litmus test for how best to implement change. Staff who are confident in, and feel supported by, their leader will feel empowered and enabled to play an active part in managing and supporting their work community through the proposed change. A consultative collegiate approach enables staff to feel not that they are looking in from the outside but that they are participants in the planned change. Their confidence in their leaders and willingness to cooperate are strengthened. It is also very important that they see messaging and actions that are joined up, consistent and clear about the aim and expected outcome.

Real-life example

Future focus, present paralysis. The governors of a relatively new school in an international setting decided they wanted to develop the school quickly into an international school for age ranges three years–eighteen years. They therefore needed to decide on the curriculum the school would offer to its high school-level students.

Based upon the school's successful curriculum delivery for the younger years, an external executive panel advised the governors to offer a prestigious international curriculum not widely known in the local community where the school was based, and the governors were persuaded to go ahead.

However, the advisers and governors had not considered the possible impact of such a decision on the wider school community, nor had they looked in sufficient depth at the factors that would be contributing to the school's growth. The school soon developed a problem with student retention. Students were being withdrawn from the school at years eight and nine, and through exit interviews with parents, it became clear why this was happening. The new curriculum had been implemented suddenly without consultation, and it emerged that parents mistrusted, and even feared, a new curriculum of which they had no experience. Parents expressed concerns that these changes would adversely affect the academic outcomes of the school, and they were unclear as to whether their children would be able to access prestigious universities and colleges based on the new qualification. They asked a pertinent question: "Why take a risk when what is in place already is working for my child?"

The school's poor communication with parents coupled with a limited recognition of, or research into, the cultural heritage of the community in which it was operating had resulted in parents responding in a way they considered right for their children. This meant moving their children to an alternative school where the parents felt they understood the curriculum and the opportunities it presented for their children. They were taking refuge in a familiar system from either an educational or a cultural perspective as they felt this would secure their children's educational potential.

There had been no forward planning by the leader of the school as to the possible negative impact of such a decision or how the school might need to respond should the changes result in students leaving. There was a complete lack of awareness as to a key step that had been missed, namely that of involving parents in such a big decision. An attempt to understand the possible impact of these changes on the school, both financially and in terms of its growth over time, had been completely neglected in the eagerness to make a change the leaders thought would benefit students.

As a result of not being sensitive to the importance of consultation or attuned to the school's context and community, the leader and governors had to revisit the situation quickly. In order to stem the exodus of students, they reviewed their decision-making in an effort to understand what precisely had gone wrong. It wasn't difficult to understand as the student numbers and parental interviews told the story. It had been an ill-informed and rashly executed decision.

Professional and honest self-review by the leader, finding the courage to share with parents, and staff the phrase, "*I got this wrong*," went a long way in persuading both the staff and some parents to give the school a second chance. The leader needed to explain in one of those deeply uncomfortable parent meeting situations how the initial decision had been taken and why it was now being reversed. Parents needed to see and trust that the benefits and well-being of the students were absolutely central to any decision and subsequent actions.

The ability to recover from an unsuccessful decision

It may take a school, or any institution, some years to recover from an ill-judged decision like the one in the above example as indeed it did in this case. In the meantime, competitors may grow and snap up more of the market share of students.

The school leader is the person who, in every respect, needs to know how to manage a consultation process and consider the expectations of the community. Decisions need to be shared together with the evidence, explaining how they were arrived at. Consultation provides an opportunity to meet parents in person and be up-front in answering the challenging questions they may pose if there is a concern. Decisions should be made only after all the facts have been gathered and relevant opinions have been considered. When full consultation has taken place and the impact of the proposed change has been understood in full, then the leader can present the eventual considered decision with confidence, using data to support and explain it.

Courage, integrity, and honesty in the face of hard decisions and potential challenges are essential leadership characteristics that need to be in evidence at such times. We have talked about this before in earlier chapters. These principles are threads throughout all leadership approaches and are worth restating. They are key elements in the profile of an authentic international leader. Remaining true to these qualities can be particularly difficult if you are a leader of a stand-alone school with minimum professional support or remote organizational support (if the owners of the school are based elsewhere, perhaps even in another country). This is when the skill of team building is vital since a strong team understands how to operate collaboratively and will support its leader, as the leader will in turn support the team. You develop skills as a group, build trust and value input from parents and the wider school community. Teamwork of this kind is the essential and solid foundation for future success.

Pause for reflection

We outlined in chapter 1 the importance of reflection as a prompt for personal development. We now look at how such reflection can strengthen leaders to address challenges, such as the uncomfortable moments they may face when making hard decisions. The position of the leader can be a lonely one, and when there is no one with whom to share thoughts and ideas, time invested in personal reflection may bear fruit in enabling the leader to find the best and most appropriate response.

Here are three key "influencers" from your time spent on self-reflection, which may nudge and challenge you to effective action:

- Your own thinking and reflections
- Your experience
- Your analysis of the situation and your decision-making for success

Think about the problematic scenario described in the example above and reflect on the following questions:

1) How would you respond to a situation like the one outlined above? What leadership strategies would you expect to use in such a situation? Do you feel you have those?
2) How would you approach a senior colleague or colleagues whose decision you disagreed with?
3) What would your biggest anxiety be, and how would you manage and address it?
4) Which skills and personal attributes that you have not yet acquired could be beneficial in this type of situation?
5) If you yourself work in education, how knowledgeable are you about the international and intercultural mix in your own school?

Credibility and courage when recruiting in international education

The need for courage, another key element found in effective leaders, as well as transparency and fairness, is likely to present itself once again during processes of staff recruitment—for example, due to school growth, recruiting new members to the team or the organization, particularly candidates from another, perhaps very different, country. This is complex. Careful recruitment methods will be needed, for example, thoughtful pacing of the interview and a sensitivity to cultural differences, choice of days and sensible timings if undertaken virtually with both parties in different countries. In international recruitment, the mix of educational and cultural experiences is likely to vary widely. A leader's credibility will be based upon cultural awareness alongside other effective recruitment strategies. If interviews are conducted entirely through a virtual platform, this overlays an additional challenge, making a candidate feel welcome!

If interviewing for positions in the Middle East or China, for example, preparation for the recruitment process has some very specific aspects. Firstly, it is important for the candidate to receive a full briefing pack ahead of the interview, outlining mandatory cultural changes/expectations and those of school protocols based on these. They need time to read and understand.

The recruiting interview process

The recruitment interview should begin with hearing about the candidates' skills and competencies and then move sensitively into exploring the cultural changes they will meet and what they feel about those. Quality time must be given over to questions. For example, some candidates may want to know what they are permitted to do in Middle East on a Friday as this is the holy day. Others may want to know about driving in China if considering a position there.

As a leader, how you interact and whether you show consideration, interest, care, and knowledge will influence an interviewee's self-confidence and their potential desire to join your team. If they feel respected and detect a genuine interest in what they themselves will bring to the school on a personal as well as a professional level, then they are more likely to accept the position if it is offered to them. It doesn't do any harm to remind yourself before you begin that you are there to listen and explore the experiences with the person you have invited. It isn't about you and selling the school for the whole time given to the interview.

Leaders must select the interviewers working alongside them skillfully too. Recruitment decisions will be lived with and judged by the rest of the staff. A well-chosen panel member will be able to offer professional knowledge as well as a personality and range of experience that can positively shape the style and direction of the interview. In a school that is culturally diverse, an international mix of colleagues from different backgrounds and cultures must be represented on the panel so that the interviewee understands the importance of inclusion and diversity within the organization and witnesses it in practice.

Careful decision-making for the best outcome

After interviews have taken place, the decision-making discussions will begin. As colleagues begin to outline the pros and cons of each candidate, the credibility of the leader will be pivotal in chairing the discussion and achieving a desirable outcome. Choosing the right person matters more than ever when you are asking a person to relocate often thousands of miles away from where they live. The appointee will be joining a new team in a new country and possibly amidst a culture with which they are unfamiliar, so a well-considered decision is essential as is good follow-up support for the successful candidate during their induction.

The international leader should be circumspect about where the discussions are taking the interview team. Some qualities may be more pivotal than others. For example, there may be evidence in favor of candidate A; however, the leader may feel that the skills of candidate C are more in line with what is needed. Candidate C may be more assertive and have the determination to get a job done in line with what is needed in the team at that time.

As a leader in this situation, if you feel that the panel is drifting toward a mistaken choice, your challenge is to summarize the team's analysis, giving credence to all the arguments, and then very clearly explain why you disagree with the drift of the discussion. You will need to be very specific in your comments, giving a clear and fair account of the additional attributes offered by candidate C, which will make this individual better suited to the role. If a consensus is impossible, you might have to exert authority and draw the discussion to a close politely but firmly with "Thank you, we are agreeing to disagree. Candidate C is the successful candidate."

Are you confident with your decision?

At a moment such as this, a leader will need to be thoroughly convinced about the requirements of the role and able to articulate clear reasons for their decision to keep their credibility intact. They would need to be in no doubt that their preferred candidate was the right fit for the team, educationally and internationally, with skills and attributes that were spot-on. This would need to be aligned with the belief that the candidate would be able to thrive in an international environment and add value to the team. The leader will need to be willing to stand by this decision, accepting that it will be tested in both specific and broad contexts. In the absence of agreement, staff will need to see openness in their leader and a willingness to explain.

It would only be over time that the members of the interview panel would come to a view about whether the leader's decision had been the right one. If time were to reveal that for a variety of reasons this was not the case, then the leader's credibility, already under the microscope, would be called into question. On the other hand, an excellent decision that demonstrated great judgment and foresight would greatly enhance the leader's credibility. These types of decisions are the backbone of great leadership.

Ram Chandran sums up the responsibilities of international leadership succinctly: "You can't be a wimp—make the tough calls" (*Harvard Business Review* [November 2013]).[5]

Pause for reflection

Chapters 2 and 3 were intended to inspire your thinking about personal leadership characteristics, especially in an international educational context. This may have delivered some surprises. Are there one or two characteristics of great leaders that you don't have in your own tool kit yet? Perhaps you have more than you first thought, in which case, are you using them to the full?

Growing and continuing to grow into a great leader is like the production of a fine tapestry where the structure (or warp thread) is knowing what your behaviors *should* be, and the actual weaving (or weft) is your work on continuing to develop them. Recognizing the experiences that have shaped your leadership attributes to date is very useful. Cultivating a high level of emotional and cultural intelligence will help you apply them at the right time and in the right place, including in international contexts.

Think about these terms and qualities in the context of your leadership:

> *Authentic:* How and in what ways do your actions match your words?
> *Visionary:* How do you know that you see the big picture?
> *Innovative:* Where is your evidence (and belief) that you can lead change imaginatively and meet the needs of students, staff, and parents?
> *Emotionally aware:* How effective are your listening skills, and how do you empower team members to act?
> *Driven by integrity:* Do you lead by example? How?

---

[5] https://hbr.org/2013/11/you-cant-be-a-wimp-make-the-tough-calls. Last accessed on 29/11/2021.

> *An effective communicator:* Do you communicate messages clearly, honestly, and succinctly without "management speak" or jargon? How do you know?
>
> *Internationally intelligent:* What leads you to believe that you are sufficiently internationally minded and alert?

It may be necessary to ask yourself these questions a few times, probing more deeply each time in order to come to an honest awareness of your professional behaviors, your strengths, and your areas for development and analyze the responses they have produced to date.

A habit of self-reflection

The greatest leaders sharpen and continue to develop their self-reflective skills, not to perfection (because that is impossible), instead, to a level that enables them to consistently self-evaluate. By this means, they maintain the highest professional leadership standards. They trust their own instincts and strive for excellence.

One very successful innovator, filmmaker, and leader, Walt Disney, is quoted as having said:

> It seems to me shallow and arrogant for any man in these times to claim he is completely self-made, that he owes all his success to his own unaided efforts. Many hands and hearts and minds generally contribute to anyone's notable achievements.

This shows a level of self-reflection and a trust in his and his team's ability to recruit good people who will make a difference. Working with them on developing their skills and abilities has enabled Disney's success to continue to grow worldwide.

The power of 3

Three quotations to irritate or maybe even inspire!

> Leaders don't just live in the moment; they look to the future and lead their organization to get there. (Twitter: @shawnbouldin [Shawn Bouldin is a principal in Victoria, British Columbia.])

> Leadership today is more than what you know. It requires the ability to adapt and respond to different circumstances and to connect with different kinds of employees. (Oliver Wyman, Global Management Consultancy Firm)

> A learning organisation is an organisation that is continually expanding its capacity to create its future. (Senge, 1990, p.14)

Three books to challenge your thinking further:

- Corbin, Carolyn. *Great Leaders See the Future First.* Chicago, 2000.
- Erikson, Tomas. *Surrounded by Idiots.* Vermilion, London, 2019.
- Van Hooser, Phillip. *Leaders Ought to Know: 11 Ground Rules for Common Sense Leadership.* Hoboken, New Jersey, 2013.

CHAPTER 4

I Am Good Enough!

As we consider leadership characteristics demonstrated by great leaders, we can probably all recall someone in a leadership position who talked a great story, however, delivered absolutely nothing as promised; someone who adopted an authoritarian style and used this as their cloak of untouchability so that they could rule the team or organization by fear. Maybe there has been someone in your own experience who managed upward (only looked to please their boss or bosses) exceptionally well or perhaps someone in authority who was quiet and ineffectual, happily being led by others in the team while drawing the leader's salary.

In the international arena, some of those behaviors may be the manifestation of personal or cultural inheritance norms gathered from experiences in other organizations or developed as the result of a leadership culture in a home country. The challenge, and indeed the route to success, in working with leaders such as these is in finding the root causes or heritage of the behaviors and then selecting the right tools to enable you to work with the person in a respectful way without the relationship becoming damaged beyond repair. You may never be able to change their leadership style, but you can, with this information, change your own behavior and, with culturally sensitive handling, bring about the developments that need to occur. If you approach with sensitivity, knowledge, and a respectful plan, it will have a positive impact upon the team you are leading as you will be seen as someone who cares about individuals and respects their heritage.

Believing in yourself

The challenge is in believing that the knowledge you have gained enables you to accomplish the necessary change without trauma. Believe in yourself. If you choose to take this as another lesson in leadership, it is well worth using the same lens to consider your own current behaviors. Your starting point needs to be *wanting* to make the difference, to make the changes needed. Others may be able to help. It is often difficult to step outside ourselves, but once we have begun to find a tentative self-belief, we can do this. We must take careful but confident steps and, of course, when appropriate, listen to others.

Autocratic leaders

People who lead teams in an autocratic manner are fundamentally poor leaders. They are both unwilling (sometimes unconsciously) and unable to empower and inspire others. Behaving differently makes an autocratic leader feel they are giving up power and that they cannot do. Autocratic leaders find it almost impossible to behave any differently as they are totally focused on themselves; they have a clear, if flawed, model in mind of how a leader should look and behave and are continually checking to see if they are meeting their own expectations. They are acting out being a leader, usually to impress those above them or to gain the status they perceive is important, moving in a direction they view as leading to continuous improvement yet moving in the *wrong* direction. The team and collaboration don't feature in their day-to-day working with colleagues. In fact, to offer an oxymoron, they are the real imposters. We discuss these imposters below identified as Type 1 Impostors. By their self-promoting actions, they hinder the work output of the team and may subconsciously, by default or even deliberately, subvert everyone's professional career development.

Autocratic and self-centered

Autocratic leaders do not find time for others unless there is something to be gained for themselves by doing so. They offer no direct professional support to aid others' learning, and their self-centered approach allows little time for listening to others' ideas or discussing their suggestions for team improvement. These leaders believe they do not need any help and instead foster a "them-and-us" mentality within the team. Often, they may find useful favorites: that is, those who strive to please them by providing key information that makes the leader look good. They bring these people into a special inner sanctum, according to themselves, a privileged status. This ensures that those out of favor are quite clearly aware of the fact.

This creates an unhealthy tense workplace where very little, if any, attention is paid to productivity toward a team goal. There is, in fact, only one person who knows where the team is going, and that is the autocratic leader who sees absolutely no need to share this information. He or she will probably communicate the tasks required, announce the timeline, and state (or threaten) what problems will arise if the tasks are not completed by a given time. The autocratic leader thrives on controlling people and may foster a culture of fear within the team as a means of motivating players to succeed and keeping everyone on their toes, anxiously watching to see what they are expected to do next.

This form of leadership is all about the culture of *me* and *my career path* with the leader consciously or unconsciously pulling the wool over the team's eyes while continuing to promote self. In some of the worst cases, autocratic leaders are not even conscious of their behavior and are oblivious of the heightened sense of frustration and even fear that is reverberating throughout the team, negatively impacting progress and success.

Is an autocratic style real leadership?

For some inexperienced colleagues on the team, this autocratic style maybe perceived as real leadership. The autocratic leader is perceived to be making decisions, moving the team on, being forceful in expecting targets to be met. Understand that this leader is a leadership imposter whose behavior encourages anything but togetherness. Autocrats do not lead, they bully. Collaboration is often quite difficult when you are amid it. It is often the case that when a brave team member (and it does take courage) points this out, the autocratic leader will push back fiercely, attributing the team's successes to their own perceived strong drive and expectations. They are also likely to turn the conversation around ferociously in criticism of the person who has questioned their style and impact. There is little or no self-awareness in this autocratic leader, and their response to this type of brave challenge is often aggressive, defensive, and a resistance to any remedial change.

It is also possible that those more senior to the leadership imposter may be unwilling to listen to any concerns or to take any action. They may have a perception that it is just too difficult or, more disappointingly, the autocratic approach may be in accordance with their intentions.

Type 1 Imposters (those who operate purely for self and believe they are immensely effective; in other words, although an oxymoron, the real imposters!) are unaware that it is necessary to focus on others and not just yourself to achieve *sustainable* success. Imposters often live in a self-delusive world, mistakenly believing they are demonstrating great leadership skills at the highest level and achieving great success based on their management of others. When success eludes them, they assume it must be someone else's fault. Type 1 imposters will seek to blame others, deflecting pressure away from themselves and excusing their own bad practice.

Once their negative leadership behaviors become apparent, imposters are generally unable to build effective teams. Team members, initially shocked and sometimes frightened by such a self-centered and egocentric approach, often pull together to support each other. Working within a team where the leader is the only one permitted to have great ideas or where he or she believes that their view, and theirs alone, should define how the team will operate can be soul destroying. There are likely to be adverse effects with team members unable to meet targets as they don't understand or feel ownership of the task. The team can quickly become dysfunctional and self-destructive, full of cliques and factions united by their collective fear or by adversity, and more concerned with surviving than working toward team goals.

Operating in a very difficult situation

What might team members do in a situation like this in order to feel better about coming to work every day and have a sense that their work matters? This type of flawed leader is the hardest one to tackle. These leaders control the team so tightly that it is incredibly hard for a frustrated team member to gain support. The unhappy staff member may try speaking to a colleague or a small group to no avail. The risk with any resistance is that it can provoke anger and retaliation from the leader, engendering a feeling within the team that the complaint has made things worse, and thus, the team's malfunction grows.

If in your leadership career you are obliged to work for a manager who exhibits this leadership style, it may be necessary to approach an even more senior leader who is prepared to listen and whom you trust. This approach still runs the risk of backlash, but if you approach the conversation in a well-prepared and unemotional way, outlining one or two concerns and their impact on the team, this could be the first step to change.

As a senior leader, if you are approached in this way, your response will require courage and an understanding that the change you seek to bring about will be a slow-release process requiring careful management of both the autocratic leader and the team members. Ultimately, your intention is for all team members to know their roles and working with a team leader they respect and whom they are beginning to trust. You will lose some team members along the way as they may leave, finding the change too slow, and you may even lose the autocratic leader due to a realization that they are damaging the organization. It's imperative that you try to fix the problem because doing nothing indicates that you have both accepted and allowed bullying and disrespectful behaviors to flourish.

How not to do it: the established autocrat

Some heads of schools (or of other organizations) believe, for mistaken reasons, that they have the right to speak to people any way they like. Some base this belief on the fact that there is no one on site to whom they are answerable and, by the same token, no one to whom unhappy or frightened staff can turn. Others take the view that their own behavior is of no consequence as it is easy to recruit replacements for any staff departing as a result of feeling upset or unvalued. If this behavior is not challenged and the leader is allowed to treat staff in a bullying manner on an ongoing basis, the person can become an established autocrat.

This kind of autocratic leader often rules through fear, exhibiting favoritism and publicly bullying staff who do not fall in with their demands. Ironically, this will not necessarily prevent the school from appearing successful in terms of student outcomes as fearful staff may work very hard to ensure they keep on the right side of this autocrat. Staff retention in such a school is likely to be poor and developing a future staffing plan difficult. When people are treated unfairly and the pressure of the work becomes unbearable, they are likely to change jobs.

One of the most insidious features of this bullying type of leader is that they inhibit their staff from complaining by instilling in them a fear of retribution. In some schools (depending on location and the national and cultural balance of the team), to challenge someone in a leadership position may be deemed disrespectful and inappropriate. Thus, the situation is perpetuated.

Talking with autocratic leaders about their leadership style often elicits the self-condoning phrases, "People know where they stand" or "I am straightforward" or "What you see is what you get."

Real-life example

Tackling an established autocrat during an appraisal. A head of school during their confidential appraisal meeting was confronted with some evidence that they were displaying bullying behaviors.

Their assessor presented concrete examples together with reports that staff were feeling intimidated and unable to discuss the issues they needed to. The individual under review became extremely angry and refused to accept this account of their leadership despite many staff complaints having been made over a period. The conversation became combative with the individual revealing an inability to reflect on their practice and acknowledge where change was necessary.

Lessons learned

This person's entrenched attitudes led the assessor to conclude that it was by now probably too late for this leader to make a fully effective and lasting change to their leadership style. The negative conversational behaviors confirmed that, in this situation, there had been two failures at senior level: firstly, the bullying issue had not been raised when it was first reported; secondly, timely support had not been offered to help the individual change their approach.

The benefits of mentoring and coaching for newly appointed leaders

A policy to provide new leaders with mentoring and coaching will bring the following benefits:

- Develop the individual in their career and help them adopt a self-reflective style
- Benefit the staff as leaders realize the importance of treating people with care and respect and keeping them well-informed
- Ensure the outcomes expected are achievable—the leader is clear what they are doing and why and can take their team with them
- Enable the individual to feel and celebrate their success as they develop a sense of purpose and grow into the role.

Managing bullying behavior before it is too late

Their performance review should not be the first time a leader becomes aware they are considered a bully. If firm examples exist, then these should be shared immediately with the person concerned and support given to them to address the issue without delay no matter how fierce or difficult the conversation involved.

Mentoring and coaching should be routinely provided when people move into leadership roles of any kind. If this does not happen, the organization stores up problems that may be difficult to solve later.

Type 2 imposters—self-doubting leaders[6] "*We all have our imposter moments. I defy any woman to say that she doesn't*" (NB: this is also true for all *leaders, regardless of gender or chosen identification*) represent a very different manifestation of the imposter syndrome. The *Cambridge Dictionary* offers a phrase to describe the inner voice of such people quite succinctly: "He felt like an imposter amongst those intelligent people, as if he had no right to be there."

These are the leaders who are incredibly reflective people, proactive in the pursuit of self-improvement, eagerly honing their existing skills—and yet lacking belief in themselves as competent leaders. They are always afraid of, somehow, being found out to be an imposter. They are self-aware and yet supremely self-critical. They believe that they are unfinished and strive to improve and refine their leadership skills.

They look at others and believe that those people are much more effective, more skilled, and more successful than themselves. An outward appearance of confidence masks the deep-seated desire to improve and the constant anxiety that one day they will be found out and found wanting. They often believe that they are not as good as people perceive them to be, which in most cases is born of a subconscious desire to find personal flaws and address them. It has been suggested that this is more often true of women in leadership posi-

---

[6] Lady Hale, *Spider Woman: A Life* (Penguin, 2021).

tions. Sheryl Sandberg in *Lean In: Women, Work, and the Will to Lead* (NYC, 2013), tells us that:

> Despite being high achievers, even experts in their fields, (some women) can't seem to shake off the sense that it is only a matter of time until they are found out for who they really are—impostors with limited skills or abilities.

In fact, if such people were able to see themselves as others see them, they would realize the quality of their leadership and the positive effect they have on their colleagues. They would also understand the need to continue as they are with the added benefit of self-belief. Is this self-doubting leader you?

Leaders who are a good fit for their team

For a leader to understand the impact of their behaviors or indeed to care enough to find out, they must first understand what makes a successful, impactful, and effective leader who generates a high-functioning team; and they need to learn how they operate in that team in order to lead it well.

Being a good fit for your team internationally usually requires an additional layer of self, cultural, organizational, and team diversity awareness. The critical aspect is to find out about the existing team's makeup: its members' national, cultural, religious, and/or political experiences, and on occasion a combination of all four. Knowing the people who work in the team and their roles and responsibilities within the school (if you are a leader in education) is the starting point. Sounds difficult? No one is claiming that international leadership is easy. Getting it right is, however, phenomenally rewarding for the leader *and* the team. When you take up a new appointment as an international leader, your new team members may be watchful, nervous, reluctant, or all three, so you will need to begin by being confident in yourself. Have belief that you can do this but also remember the importance of taking things one step at a time.

Do your homework

Time spent on planning is never wasted. If new staff have been appointed or existing staff promoted, treat the interview and appointment process as a learning opportunity to familiarize yourself with their CVs (résumés), combining proactive research with the benefits of professional intuition or "gut feeling" gained from earlier experience. Performance in the job and the social getting-to-know-you aspects during the first few weeks will be vital in building a professional relationship with the new appointees. Be led by what you are experiencing. For example, after the first group meeting, decide whether individual one-to-ones would be the best next step or whether another group meeting will be necessary to build the camaraderie. Be confident in your ability to read the team but go cautiously. They will be looking to you for direction, and you are looking to them to be collaborators. No amount of sophisticated professional development opportunities can take the place of the personal finding-out process.

None of this is time wasted; on the contrary, it is quite explicitly time well spent. Team members begin to feel valued for who they are on a personal level and for the skills and attributes they bring to the leader and the team. This perceptiveness about what an individual brings indicates that decisions will be made based on attributes and skills, rather than being adversely influenced by ad hoc views about cultural origins, previous practices, or by unconscious bias. Bear in mind that everyone is on a learning curve: it is simply that you are taking the lead in showing confidently that you are willing to hear, learn, reflect, and act.

The importance of two-way relationships

Relationship building is a first stage *must* for great leaders seeking to build successful teams. There is, of course, a need for care and attention in the forward planning of team meetings or social gatherings. Beyond the obvious dietary needs and dress code mandates, it will help to know in advance a little more about the team members and their basic preferences, likes and dislikes. Such preparation will show them that you have taken the time to find out about them and that they matter to you. It will also provide you with insights if some team members choose not to attend, for example, due to a lack of social confidence. Time spent on understanding your team's makeup and their characteristics can go a long way toward running a successful event and should set you on course for longer-term buy-in of team members. Over many years, we have heard people make remarks that are variations of "they took the time to ask about me, not just about the job."

Working with autocratic or self-doubting leaders

The examples from real situations in this chapter provide evidence of where leadership has failed to live up to its name and why.

Many type 1 imposters (autocrats) have been unable or unwilling to identify individuals' potential. They have not been able to motivate or inspire their teams to deliver fully what is expected of them because of an inability to be empathetic to, or aware of, the beliefs and practices of their diverse staff and use this awareness to advantage. They are too self-focused, self-absorbed, and self-promoting. Caligula, a Roman emperor, was the first to be assassinated due to his continued increase of personal power. His reign was defined by creating ambitious projects that would only benefit himself. In short, type 1 imposters completely lack the appropriate skills to be judged as good or great leaders.

The behaviors of a type 1 imposter are likely to lead their team members to develop a mutual support network, leaving the imposter isolated and, within a short space of time, unable to dictate how the team will operate. The imposter may not be aware in the beginning that this is happening until they begin to feel frustrated, and their already negative behaviors give way to more extreme demands as they struggle to reassert authority and try to achieve their goals.

This can be apparent very quickly in international settings where a leader, new to international working, has been overconfident in their skills or their previous experience, showing no interest in or intent to understand the cultural setting within which they are now operating. This often results in frustration when the team hasn't responded to the expected demands. Autocratic leaders do not reflect on which of their actions or omissions might be hindering progress since they have no conception that any of the problems may be their own fault. They often resort to an even more demanding approach, pushing down hard on team members and setting even more unachievable targets. Harsh pronouncements about expectations and deadlines are the hallmarks of a type 1 imposter. They are locked in a vicious circle of poor leadership and the inability to perceive even basic facts about where they are going wrong.

What effective leaders know

Conversely, a good leader acquires a sound knowledge of others, their strengths and skills, and deploys staff in a considered way, thus avoiding disgruntlement or downright adversarial responses. They set the team up for success. Good leaders are able to position "round pegs in round holes." This demonstrates people comfortable in their position, understanding the demands of the role and work well to achieve the expected outcomes. To use a further metaphor, they plant individuals in soil where there is enough space for them to grow and expand their reach.

Self-doubting leaders can also fail in their leadership intentions. In this case, as a result of questioning their own skills too publicly and too frequently. Transparency and self-awareness are essential qualities of leadership, yet there is a balance to be achieved. Teams do not benefit from seeing their leader in a spiral of self-doubt or, more damaging still, constantly seeking validation by pleading for feedback in a self-deprecatory manner.

Questions to ask here if you feel either description resonates with you are:

- In what ways am I effective? How do I know?
- Was my decision the right one? How do I know?
- What might show me that I am *not* doing this correctly?
- Did I verge toward type 1 autocratic, imposter characteristics? If yes, what next?

Team members are looking for collaboration, but ultimately, they need and want a leader who leads. Too much public self-doubt can be just as detrimental to the team as the type 1 leader's approach.

Developing diverse teams

The success of high-performing international teams is grounded in the ability of the leader and team members to:

- ✓ Have respect for and knowledge of each other's personal, professional, and cultural behaviors and expectations
- ✓ Be flexible and respond rapidly and positively to change, challenging either the status quo or the reason for change appropriately—even if this is uncomfortable
- ✓ Be responsive to sensitivities and able to gauge the buy-in and morale of other team members
- ✓ Build camaraderie, recognizing that different personalities, nationalities, and cultural backgrounds may mean that people respond differently in social or interactive situations
- ✓ Express themselves clearly and respectfully to others
- ✓ Be passionate and committed to the team's vision and mission, understanding the implications of both, and committed to delivering
- ✓ Detach themselves from their own personal ideas and solutions
- ✓ Be able to perform the tasks needed by the team
- ✓ Actively listen to each other and work collaboratively for the common good
- ✓ Be positive and supportive of team decisions regardless of how they felt during the decision-making process

People in leadership positions who cannot inspire, motivate, and develop a group of people to achieve the capabilities above, who are committed mainly to the "me" principle of leadership, are simply not able to work within a team to create anything. Real, dynamic "teamness" will evade them, as within a team operating like this, confusion and chaos will thrive. We have all heard or used the expression, "There is no *I* in team." Sadly, on many occasions, there *is E* for ego!

How not to do it

Type 1 and 2 dysfunctional teams. Teams led by type 1 and type 2 imposters fail when or because:

- There is one leader who is there to tell and not ask.
- The leader is unwilling to collaborate.
- There are people with the wrong skill set.
- There is one absolute resister.
- Differing opinions are allowed to be discussed incessantly.
- Either everything is allowed to be negotiable or nothing is.
- There is a no action team in place.
- There is an unwillingness to face facts.
- Interpersonal misunderstandings and miscues exist.

Effective recruitment for international education settings

Recruitment is a recurring theme as appointing leaders of international schools (principals, directors, or administrators) is a challenging task and getting it right is paramount to the team's success. The overall leader is, of course, a key player in the school's success at all levels. The process of selection at present remains generally focused on trial by interview often involving parents, staff, students, board members, owners, and more. When able, there can be in-person "trial by etiquette," i.e., the multifarious coffees and dinners. Recently a new layer of "trial by digital" has joined the fray. Digital communication has been a feature of many international interview processes for some time, where travel has been either prohibitively expensive in time or cost for interviewees or organizations. The digital interview or informal chat has stepped into its own now. Most of us are sensitive to the challenges of interviews and would-be social occasions for which we summon up a heightened state of awareness and the desire to impress; this is just as much the case with digital encounters as with traditional ones.

The importance of a diverse, balanced recruitment panel

Few schools consider the mix of people represented on such professional panels. Schools rarely share suitable preinterview information about the candidates. This is based on giving due consideration to protection of sensitive data; however, information that could usefully be shared includes previous international experience and the type of organization where the candidate gained their current or previous experience in education. Such thorough preparation can aid the panel in making the right decision at the end of the process, instead of feeling pressured into making a choice based on only some of the necessary information. A rogue question from an ill-informed panel member has the potential to undermine the credibility of the panel and change the direction of the decision.

A well-balanced panel will not just be looking for one set of attributes, nor will it have one set of cultural expectations. It might be impressive to meet an interviewee who is a talented communicator on the philosophy of education, has great eye contact, and looks relaxed and engaged (virtually or in person). These physical and verbal cues can be very persuasive to a board or panel searching for a great communicator to enhance the school's reputation. These interviewee skills and attitude is giving a message that says, "I am the right choice. Choose me." However, they are no guarantee that the candidate possesses other characteristics necessary to the makeup of an effective leader in this context, such as emotional intelligence or international mindedness. Remember also that not everyone will interpret body language the same way.

Real-life example

When appearances are deceptive. An experienced director of education had been focused on reviewing the quality of leadership and student outcomes across schools, including the line management of heads of schools. One school was causing an executive team great concern. Specifically, poor student outcomes were observed in the high school, and there had been an increasing number of parental concerns about the effectiveness of the school leader. However, on termly visits to the school, the head of school ably led detailed conversations about the work of the school and the progress being made, implying that all was well. It seemed, through conversation and a plethora of written evidence, that everything was fine. It seemed that strategic decisions were being implemented to improve learning. On leaving the school after each visit, the director was convinced that the right measures were on track for the appropriate changes to be swiftly made.

However, complaints continued to accumulate, and the end-of-year external exam results showed an unacceptably low number of students achieving their predicted grades. It was a challenge to work out why there had been no real progress or identifiable success. A swift visit followed, the only agenda item being "What happened?"

Everyone settled down and unpicked the actions in minute detail. The director spoke with staff about communications and involvement in the change process. It became clear that while the school leader had put in long hours of determined and diligent work to create a strategic plan focused on need and understood what needed to be done, no one else had been involved in the decision-making process, nor had the staff been made aware of the issues raised about the school's lack of progress and parental concerns. The school leader's plan was delivered to middle leaders via their separate staff room pigeonholes with no collective team discussion of any kind. A review date was set for six months later, and that was that!

Key messages had failed to be effectively communicated, nor was their importance made obvious. No one checked that team members understood what their individual roles in the improvement process should be.

The director of education, the external quality reviewer, had been inadvertently misled by the school leader, who, despite the best of intentions, had been ineffectual. During the monitoring conversations, the director of education had not dug deep enough to explore how the school leader was interacting with the staff to implement necessary changes.

Action taken. Following these discoveries, lengthy professional conversations took place to verify that the plans for improvement were indeed suitably focused and, if well implemented, capable of bringing about the required changes. The challenge then was to help the leader see why the action of simply distributing the written plan would not automatically lead to the desired changes occurring. It was difficult for this leader to understand what appeared as a dichotomy: positive discussions around leadership and learning and a clear understanding of the school's situation. Yet, on the other hand, an inability to interact with staff and seek their views, draw out their ideas, explain the situation they were in, and communicate how, together with the actions agreed, they could turn the school around.

The head of school had felt that there wasn't time for this process and that staff would be pleased not to have to be bothered with this task. The discussions around engagement, ownership, and responsibility that the director of education now facilitated were lengthy and not immediately successful. The head of school showed some acceptance that staff would have more ownership in the plan if they were involved but also came back with a passionate and articulate riposte about the pace and pressure of life in school that made these conversations about strategic plans a luxury, rather than the key drivers of school improvement that they absolutely should be.

Leaders who "manage upward"

There are many people we meet in organizations who are skillful in managing upward. They see those above them in the hierarchy as those they must always impress. They believe that increasing their power and responsibility will be achieved by connecting *only* with those senior to them; their energies are focused on being upwardly mobile in terms of their own career and status and pay scant attention to helping their team achieve their goals both team related and personal.

People who behave in this way want to be noticed by their senior managers in order to metaphorically climb the company ladder and achieve a higher, more powerful status. They do not mind whom they inconvenience or marginalize in order to get there. Many leaders are adept at conducting themselves in this way without anyone in their team noticing it or feeling marginalized by it. There are, however, occasions when such behavior, even when normalized within a team, can become seriously damaging.

There have been instances in international schools where new staff arrive with a deep-seated legacy from a previous school system or group where such behavior of working to impress those above you have been actively encouraged. For example, a local ministry of education might have instructed, "Here are the five things you must do to be successful," so the colleague begins to work on these to please the leader above them. A private school owner might have said, "I want you to increase the number of students in your classes," and the leader works solely on fulfilling this requirement where there may have been other more important issues to tackle first.

Two wrongs do not make a right

There are many examples of school leaders who, aggrieved at a decision taken at director level, have seen fit to bypass the protocols of the school and have demanded to speak to the chair of the board (or chair of governors, depending on the type of school and country). This bombastic tactic contravenes the correct professional approach, which is to discuss the issue with the appropriate director first. This enables:

- The relevant director to gain a fuller understanding of the issue
- The school leader to explain courteously what it is they do not like and why
- Both parties to work out what the follow-up actions will be.

This approach of bypassing the responsible decision-maker above them is often used by leaders who consider themselves very important and powerful and thus entitled to influence their senior colleagues. It can sometimes, though, lead to their removal. A leader who does this seeks to gain the ear of one influential person (seeking a privileged status with them) while sidelining others who may have more direct responsibility to support and help.

Real-life example

Covert behavior creates a culture of fear. A head of school was overheard by the director of education speaking in an aggressive and offensive manner to a more junior colleague during a phone call. The junior colleague was clearly seen as an unimportant subordinate rather than a valued member of staff. The director of education asked for the phone to be handed over to her and took over the call, demonstrating an appropriate manner in which courtesy was front and center. This action resulted in the head of school changing their approach dramatically.

The director of education also took the opportunity to make a personal visit to the school and discuss the conversation she had overheard. Unfortunately, the "managing upward" continued but more carefully and out of earshot, with an entrenched belief that the approach that had been used was the right one and effective no matter what anyone else said. This type of leader may simply adjust their tactics when challenged and continue to use it. While leading by example can be effective, bringing about permanent changes in attitudes can be a long-term project requiring persistent work.

Action taken. Addressing the issue more widely across the heads of schools throughout the organization was difficult and required courage. Many heads of schools believed they were exempt from criticism as they had the ear of the board (that is, they felt they were in a close collaboration with them). It was troubling to discover that key board members were encouraging this attitude in the mistaken belief that doing so would present a valid opportunity to learn more about problematic issues at the school. In fact, this undercover intelligence achieved the exact opposite, undermining the unity and integrity of the school's leadership. The board members had given no thought to how they might use the covertly obtained information to bring about improvement. In the resultant atmosphere, many colleagues who worked for these heads became fearful, both about the continuation of their contracts and about how to cope with day-to-day experiences and challenges.

Staff reported poor behaviors, little progress in tackling problems, and exceptionally low levels of respect for all colleagues emanating from the leadership. Leaders who use these covert tactics for their own benefit will try to justify it to themselves and others, but this is self-delusion. It must be clearly stated: covert, oppressive behavior is *bullying* behavior.

Taking decisive action in a situation can bring about immediate improvement; however, for an enduring cultural change, you must address it over time. Turning a blind eye and hoping it will go away is obviously ineffectual. Instead, you need to take the following actions. This list refers to actions a leader may take when being very badly managed by the senior leader to whom they report to or a team member in a very poorly led team. You will be one or the other at some point in your career.

1) Identify the real issues
2) Consider all facts
3) Check out with trusted colleagues whether your observations are accurate
4) Consider ways of bringing your findings to the leader's attention
5) Consider ways in which, within your team, you can work to improve your own area of work and the outcomes that you and the team want to achieve. If you feel this is not possible without serious impact on yours or others' careers, then understand together and do not feel guilty that, on this occasion, you are choosing to be pragmatic and doing what you can. This is okay!

How not to do it: Long-distance leadership

There is also the type of leader who opts for the ineffective style of long-distance leadership. Often these people have developed, or have been given, an inflated view of their position. They believe that, provided they give out orders or expect others to make decisions (pseudo-collaborative leadership), everything will be fine. They do not realize this style results in a confused and fractured team. Often, such leaders are oblivious of the adverse impact that this flawed leadership style is having on the team. Only when the fallout begins and problems manifest do they realize the need to address their actions if indeed there is time to do so at this stage. In most cases, this critical point is usually reached as a result of staff requesting external support as things go badly wrong.

Have a think!

This is your time again for reflection. It is likely that you have come across at least one example of the imposter syndrome in your working life to date or have encountered some of the other flawed leadership styles discussed in this chapter. As you reflect on the different flawed leadership styles you have read about, can you identify any of the not-so-great characteristics in yourself?

Think about the real-life examples in this chapter. Answer the following questions honestly about yourself (you don't have to share your answers with anyone!).

- Would your response to these real-life situations have been different? If so, how? Would your response have worked better? Is this process helping you define your own leadership style?
- If faced with this situation after reading this chapter, would you address the issue confidently? What would be your very first step?

- Can you identify any situations you have faced in which you took confident actions that made a difference? What empowered you to take these successful actions?
- If you are aware of having any of the characteristics of the flawed leaders in this chapter, does this behavior conceal something deeper that you need to address? What first steps can you take to bring yourself back on track and develop a more self-assured and effectual leadership style?

When you have finished this reflection, take the time now to celebrate what you *know* you are good at and celebrate the fact that the negative imposter syndrome approach does not sit with you.

The power of 3

Three quotations to ponder:

> Recognizing that you are truly in over your head is a positive first step—and tactically, it's probably better to recognize this deficit before your boss does! (Twitter: @Dougblackie)

> It doesn't matter how intelligent, affable, persuasive, or savvy a person is, if they are prone to rationalizing unethical behaviour based upon current or future needs, they will eventually fall prey to their own undoing. (Adeola Babatunde, *Are you a Leader?*)

> People ask the difference between a leader and a boss. The leader leads, and the boss drives. (Theodore Roosevelt, Twenty-Sixth President of the United States)

Three books to challenge your thinking further:

- DeVries, Kets, and F. R. Manfred. *Leaders, Fools, and Imposters: Essays on the Psychology of Leadership.* Hoboken, New Jersey, 1993.
- Caslen, Robert L., Jr., and Michael Matthews. *"The Character Edge": Leading and Winning with Integrity.* Macmillan, 2020.
- Hadeed, Kristen, and Simon Sinek. *Permission to Screw Up.* Portfolio, 2017.

CHAPTER 5

Building and Leading Diverse and Successful Teams

In chapter 3, we explored the characteristics, dispositions, and behaviors of people who are on the trajectory to become great leaders or are there already. In chapter 4, we also identified evidence that indicates the style of those who are less likely to get there and looked at what they need to do differently.

This chapter, which is applicable in almost any leadership context, considers the importance of diversity, equality, and inclusion in the workplace whilst also looking at the challenges of building effective teams, even when this involves difficult decisions and processes.

A diverse team is a flexible and capable one

The premise that people of all races, cultures, genders, and beliefs should be treated with equity and fairness is fundamental for all high-performing organizations and a basic expectation for their staff. Leadership at all levels accelerates positively when this principle is at the heart of the organizational culture and basic human rights are embedded into everyday practice.

The guidance in this chapter only becomes contentious if the leader is working in an organization or country (there are some) where it is considered unacceptable for a leader to accept and address fallibility, question his or her own judgment, and/or be seen to have made an error. That should not deter leaders from personal self-reflection and acting to improve performance when the opportunity to do so presents itself.

As we increase our understanding of the positive impact that behaviors promoting diversity, equality, and inclusion have on individuals and teams in general, we will also focus more sharply on how these behaviors affect team culture in an international setting. In an international context, it is important to identify what the most potentially impactful leadership needs of your team are. It is also useful to determine whether teams work differently in an international setting. What different cultural norms need to be acknowledged and adhered to? What may be the different legal requirements that need to be understood and followed, e.g., business or personal tax situations? What are the religious beliefs (and interpretations of religious practices and customs) to be respected and adhered to during a working day or week?

If you are a team leader, you need to get comfortable with addressing the question of unconscious bias since a team or organization will only thrive when all seek conversations that will inform your actions, enabling you to hear, address, and respond to the needs of the diverse community in which you work. Seeking information and views may come from students, parents, or the local community at large. Seeing a leader authentically interested in understanding how people are treated and actively setting about to improve this gains respect quickly and often garners the support of others. This doesn't mean that everything asked must happen; rather, careful consideration is given to requests, and when a decision is made, reasons are provided as to why it is yes or no. Actions speak more loudly than words and will be noted both by those within the organization and by outside observers. If unconscious bias is acknowledged, the actions the leadership takes to minimize and eradicate it are crucial to establishing a diverse valued community. The question on everyone's lips will be, "Is this a diverse team built on mutual respect and with the best interests of the community at its heart?"

What makes you a leader who respects diversity?

There are leaders who genuinely believe that they are leading well without any awareness that what they say, or say they do, is not what they *actually* do. Simply saying that you are a good leader, respectful of cultural differences, with equality at the heart of your practice is futile if you know deep down that you do not live this in practice. Such self-delusion is detrimental to your own professional growth and hinders the growth and trust of the team as people are quick to detect a lack of authenticity. To avoid these pitfalls, act on your words. Be self-aware. Face up to and address personal misconceptions. Live by sound principles seen in your actions. Attention to diversity, equality, and inclusion must be something that you actively demonstrate and expect to be demonstrated by your team. This may be a time when external professional development, books read, or videos watched to see may be needed to support actual change and enable people to experience the impact of unconscious bias for example and receive expert guidance to set about the journey of improvement.

Don't worry if up until this section of the book, you had not realized that some of your leadership behaviors were non-inclusive with perhaps a negative effect on the team. You don't have to be one of the many people who lead without ever being aware that self-delusion is sabotaging their success. Leaders who lack emotional intelligence and self-awareness are unwittingly self-absorbed and arrogantly believe that they are doing a great job at all times on all issues, even though they are not. Instead, you can start to change any negative behaviors today, armed with the new knowledge gained in this chapter. However, you must believe that a diverse community enriches the outcomes for all members that both equality and equity are embedded in your practice because you believe in it and that the active inclusion of people from different backgrounds, beliefs, and different skills is what makes your team *great!*

The book [7] *Everyday Bias: Identifying and Navigating Unconscious Judgments in Our Daily Lives* by Howard J. Ross is worthy of a read at this point.

Managing diverse teams in international contexts

The complexities and specific needs of teams in international contexts present challenges. The leadership behaviors that will help you and your team succeed depend on you developing the self-awareness to learn how to behave in appropriate ways at specific times, meeting the needs of the context and the circumstances in which you find yourself. Teams want to trust, believe in, and be proud of their leader and to know that their leader reciprocates these feelings.

In terms of management techniques and professional relationships, they want their leader to:

- Be kind and behave respectfully toward all members of the team
- Publicly recognize the skills and attributes within the team
- Take time to praise and thank staff authentically
- Be alert to stresses, tensions, or personal issues and respond swiftly and empathetically
- Know "who" each individual is in addition to "what" they represent in their role
- Metaphorically "roll up their sleeves" and "get right into it" when the need arises (before a small problem becomes a major issue)
- Break down cliques/factions or heal divisions when these arise within the team.

---

[7] Howard J. Ross, *Everyday Bias: Identifying and Navigating Unconscious Judgments in Our Daily Lives* (Rowan and Littlefield, July 2020).

In terms of organization-level strategic management and proactive leadership, they want their leader to:

- Have integrity
- Articulate the organization's vision and set out expected behaviors
- Be clear about the team's collective priorities
- Be clear and direct in communicating individual responsibilities and accountabilities
- Make decisions, including tough decisions when necessary, ensuring fairness prevails
- Ensure any terminology is unambiguously translated or presented so that it will be clearly understood (for example, in Mandarin, the words "resilience" and "respect" have many equivalents and so careful thought is needed in translating).

Considerate behaviors are particularly pertinent in an international school-based context: a necessary requirement to engender a sense of collegiality in a diverse staff. By "considerate," we mean genuinely caring behaviors that indicate authentic respect for the cultures represented within the team.

The "behaviors" list may seem daunting. A useful starting point is to identify and give yourself credit for any of those behaviors that are already part of your leadership style. Having done so, now think about the ones that you need to work on. Remember, by accepting the potential positive impact of these behaviors, you are also acknowledging what you do not want to experience from others, traits such as cynicism, disrespect, or ignorance of your sensitivities.

People-centered, empathetic leadership

Obviously, offering and successfully implementing an international education is a fundamental expectation of a leader in an international school. To achieve this, strong, effective, and people-centered leadership is critical.

So...if a people-centered approach is the foundation for effective and sustainable internal and external (community) relationships, how do you achieve it? An effective leader knows that this must be genuine and never rushed. Thoughtful, honest, and respectful interactions enable a school leader to develop a diverse group of staff whose background, skills, and cultural experiences truly add value. You don't have to achieve this immediately; a good approach is to develop a plan that will take a few weeks or months to bring to fruition. Identify days and times when you will meet, plan, or discuss things with your team and dates when you will review decisions before implementing them. Do *not* rush, instead collaborate with purpose. Build those relationships. You can see quickly if the plan is working when, amongst the whole staff community, there starts to be a tangible ethos of belonging, a sense of ownership of the school's culture, and a sense of accountability demonstrated in everyday situations.

Leaders of international schools, probably more than those of any other kind of school, must put maximum time and effort into the staff-induction process and the integration of new staff into the team from both a cultural and a structural perspective. This will not be achieved simply by implementation of the school's policies, practices, and procedures or by limiting the staff induction period to two weeks prior to the beginning of term. Some staff may have undergone the stress of travelling to an unfamiliar country and will be encountering new work and cultural expectations. Therefore, the wise international leader plans a holistic twelve-month induction process (rather than a short induction or single event) that involves coaching, career mentors or "buddies," regular one-on-ones, and social events. This leader will be alert to the fact that some colleagues may be shy or not comfortable going to social events, may have specific cultural or religious needs to be addressed and respected, and there may be many other reasons for people's responses to and participation in social events. You need to be sensitive to indications of any such discomfort or reactions.

Even the most seasoned international travelers or "global nomads" go through periods of homesickness, unhappiness, anxiety, sadness, doubt, and fear. This can be exacerbated if no one in their new work location seems aware of the festivals, key events, national days, or seasonal traditions of their home country. When staff are not able to travel home at key holiday points in their own cultural or national year, owing to the school calendar, it is important for leaders to plan something special for them to acknowledge the event and reduce the stress and disappointment felt. This is where empathy is an invaluable attribute, especially when leading to a thoughtful action.

Real-life example

Inclusion is a feeling. A conversation with a very experienced leader spotlighted an occasion when she had felt the "outsider syndrome." While sharing her excitement that her small daughter, at an international school in the Middle East, would be enjoying a Diwali celebration in her class, this leader recalled the sadness and sense of exclusion that she herself had felt early in her international teaching career on being away from her home country at Diwali. No one had mentioned or even recognized that this was a very special time for her. Even now, many years later, the memory of this was still upsetting. Inclusion, it is true to say, is a feeling and so, by default, is exclusion deliberate or not?

Maya Angelou encapsulated this: "I've learned that people will forget what you said, people will forget what you did, but people will never forget how you made them feel."

Building a team with the right skills and attributes

When you are putting a team together or taking over an established team, there are usually difficult decisions to be made. How you handle these will determine your success. Being clear about the behaviors and attitudes you want to see from your staff is just as important as ensuring that they have relevant skills and experience.

If you have inherited your team, your first challenge is to assess the balance of skills and attributes that exists within it. A sensitively conducted team talent review simply involves being aware of the skills, attributes, and attitudes that you require and comparing this list with those that you have observed. Once you have done this, the very significant challenge is how to manage any necessary training needs or indeed changes of personnel within the team to ensure success. Planning necessary changes will take time and will require confidential discussions with key team members. It is never easy to have to inform someone that they no longer have a role or are being moved to a different team because of the huge impact of the decision on that person's life. While this human resource practice may not be allowed in some countries, it is still practiced in many. There are times when it must be done for the growth and improvement of the team. Make sure that you follow correct procedures and observe all legal requirements, as well as be careful to handle the situation sensitively on a personal level.

The first time you do this, and on all subsequent occasions, you will need to draw on your reserves of professional courage. As all skilled leaders know, professional courage must be a bottomless resource as it will be needed and relied upon many times throughout your career. You will learn over time how to "dig deep" and tap into it however difficult this may seem at first. Any recipient of negative news wants it to be delivered swiftly, honestly, and fairly no matter how upset or angry it may make them feel. Unwelcome news is not something that should be leaked and talked about for days by team members before action is taken. The person to whom the news pertains must be the first to hear it, and it must be delivered in a considerate but firm (not harsh) way. Consider, decide, plan, act.

Stepping up with courage when change is needed

With reference to the difficult task of team restructuring, many of us will have heard someone say, "This is above my pay grade. It isn't my job!" On the contrary, if a team must be restructured and you are leading the team, then it certainly *is* part of your job. It is a matter not of pay, it is one of responsibility. If this occurs, then as team leader, you are likely to be responsible for:

- Managing the change process effectively
- Enabling others to know and understand their role in the process
- Communicating to individuals in a timely and sensitive manner how they will be affected
- Creating a team that does what it takes to get the task done.

Delegating these change-management responsibilities is not an option. Sharing information about the process openly is essential, and the right communication methods and narratives are important. The leader must motivate and inspire the team to take on board what is required for them to be successful. To enable everyone to face, embrace, participate in, and adapt to change, it's critical to ensure that there is full engagement. Your briefings as leader will need to be encouraging, challenging, and supportive in the right balance. Things must be done properly with no shortcuts. It is important to help team members understand that you are all in this together.

Real-life example

A tale of courage and cowardice. A leader was involved in restructuring an enormous organization made up of many facilities and people. Disappointingly, one very senior colleague made it clear that they were *not keen* at all to step up and share this responsibility. So single-handedly, this person established a series of weekly information meetings for all staff. Timings were thoughtfully planned to suit the schedules of day and evening workers. At first, the sessions were tense as question after question rained down about impact and timing. However, as this major change task unfolded and further meetings took place, the sense of disquiet eased. People felt informed *personally*. If they could not attend a meeting, they knew that their follow-up email requesting information would be answered honestly and swiftly. Despite having been left to manage the process alone, this leader understood the importance of good communication and planned for it.

After a nine-month program of consultation and feedback, the major restructure was agreed. Final decisions were shared and implemented with very little external legal intervention or unrest among the staff.

Now that the work had been successfully completed, some of the senior personnel who had been passive during the process now clambered to take credit. This approach of waiting to see what happened before acknowledging any responsibility was blatant enough to make some people query why no other senior colleagues had been present at the weekly briefings.

Clearly, the whole process had relied on the cognitive and personal strength of one individual who had persevered without support. Staff expressed respect and genuine concern for the person who had walked alongside them throughout this time of significant change. A team had grown out of disparate, dispirited, and anxious human beings. One person's courage and clarity had enabled something important to happen, yet those with whom they had shared the journey were the actual staff that they consulted, not the senior colleagues who should have taken responsibility and supported the strategic process and out of cowardice and egocentricity ("I can't be seen to be wrong") did not.

Pause for reflection

This chapter should have encouraged you to think about some of the challenges you may face as a team leader. As a leader, your most critical task is to model and encourage open and honest communication appropriate to the context no matter how unpleasant or uncomfortable the topic. Reflect again on the example above:

What did this leader do well?
What do you think was the most difficult part of the process?
How might *you* have handled this?
What may be the professional skills to help you to prepare for similar situations?

Now that you are really focusing on your own leadership attributes through deep personal analysis, take time to identify the aspect that has been the biggest surprise regarding your own positive skills, attributes, and behaviors. What are your achievements to date as a successful leader? What additional skill or attribute would you find especially useful to work on next?

The power of 3

Three quotations to consider:

> Try not to become a man of success but rather try to become a man of value. (Albert Einstein)

> Behavior is the mirror in which we can display our image. (Mahatma Gandhi)

> Eating words has never given me indigestion. (Sir Winston Churchill)

Three books to challenge your thinking further:

- Sinek, Simon. *Leaders Eat Last: Why Some Teams Pull Together and Others Don't.* London, 2017.
- Shapiro, Joan Poliner, and Jacqueline Anne Stefkovich. *Ethical Leadership and Decision-Making in Education: Applying Theoretical Perspectives to Complex Dilemmas,* fourth edition. Abingdon, UK, 2016.
- Ford, Debbie. *Why Good People Do Bad Things: How to Stop Being Your Own Worst Enemy.* New York: HarperCollins Publishers, 2009.

CHAPTER 6

Communications: The Essence of Success

When you take a journey by train, subway, boat, or plane, it can be surprising and perhaps fascinating to hear conversations and observe those around you. As a result of mobile technology and the inconsiderate or unaware behavior of some fellow travelers, you sometimes become party to private or intimate conversation, whether you want to or not. You may overhear information never meant for public consumption, the speaker being focused only on the unseen person they are talking to and apparently paying no heed to the adage that "careless talk costs lives"—or at least that those indiscretions could have repercussions. Such information as the names of organizations, people's medical details (and potentially libelous hearsay!) is carelessly shared with complete strangers. This is not how you want to operate. Being aware of your surroundings always is a must.

The importance of confidentiality

A person should not be carelessly sharing private or confidential information, least of all with complete strangers while traveling on public transport. Communications and confidentiality sit side by side as assessing the context in which you are having the conversation determines what can or should be said and what should not. You can't communicate effectively until you are sure what information is, and is not, appropriate for you to share. In the public transport example above, people disclose information that they shouldn't because of a false confidence that those around them are not listening, are engaged in something else, or don't care. However, there is certainly no guarantee that this is the case; on the contrary, even the most moral person is likely to feel at least some fascination in overhearing juicy bits of other people's lives.

How you communicate, paying attention to where you are, is the essence of a thoughtful leader who acts with integrity. Confidentiality means you care about *what* you say, *when* you say it, and to *whom*.

It is not acceptable, following a difficult conversation with an employee, to pick up your phone in a public area and share the content of this conversation openly with your line manager or, worse, your partner or friend. If you have confirmed that the conversation will be confidential, then you have a duty to ensure it stays that way. Even if you have not confirmed this, you still need to develop sufficient professional judgment to recognize confidential information when you hear it and make sure that you respect the other person's privacy. You only have one shot at this as a leader because if any colleague finds you chatting openly about a confidential conversation, even if with good intent, then your reputation as someone who can be trusted and respected will be ruined. You cannot claw back an unguarded moment. You can, most certainly, guard against it.

Confidentiality

Confidential means just that. If you think about it from the other person's point of view, you can see why. Imagine a situation where you find your private or personal concerns being talked about in a casual or derogatory manner. Or imagine that your private information was the subject of a humorous chat amongst colleagues. Reflect how you would feel. Most people would find that situation hurtful and demeaning, even devastating. Would you want that for others? Leaders who act with integrity never put their colleagues in this position. The only exception is when you need to stop a colleague doing something in the moment, and the timing is too important for the matter to remain confidential. Even in this situation, you should be as discreet as possible and avoid unnecessarily shaming the person, for example, with a public reproach such as "I warned you about this last week, remember?" You would only share necessary information in a sensitive manner with the person who needed to act on it. This is entirely different from sharing over a cup of coffee. Great leaders don't participate in gossip or encourage it, knowing the damage it can inflict on the person and the team.

To improve your communications, understand how they work

No analysis or discussion around leadership can occur without stressing the fundamental importance of effective communication. How else can we lead if we can't share with people the "what" and "how"? We have covered this area in previous chapters; however, regular revision, a pause for reflection is a reminder of how important this is as you grow as a leader.

At this stage of your development journey, you should now be able to recognize desirable leadership characteristics. You will have a greater perception of your own current leadership style, your strengths, and any areas you need to work on. You should also celebrate how far you have progressed in your understanding of self, of teams, and how to take account of individual needs and the importance of this. You will have reflected on how diversity benefits the team overall. It naturally follows that your next big step is to review the quality of your communications and consider if they can be improved.

Pause for thought

Improving our powers of communication at all levels and in all forms enables us to build better relationships, share information appropriately, achieve buy-in from staff, and open the doors to business excellence. Working on developing this is an important stage in your journey, and before embarking on it, you may need to spend some time analyzing how communications take place within your organization currently. Think about the following questions:

- How is shared information received by others? Is it received the way it was intended it to be?
- If people are reading the information, are they understanding it fully? What is the evidence of success?
- When notes of a meeting or memos are sent out to ensure everyone is informed of a decision, does everyone read them and understand them?
- How many people might be deleting emailed notes without reading them? How would you find this out sensitively as it could be a critical area to work on/improve?
- What do people think about the current methods of communication? In what ways are they effective? What might be a better way to do it?
- How are you seeking colleagues' views to aid improvement?

Reflect on your answers. In what ways might they reveal why your team has perhaps been slow to respond to actions you thought had been agreed at meetings?

This is an important exercise in discovering what works and what doesn't before a leader, with team involvement, decides on what changes are necessary to improve communications. You need colleagues' assistance to hear the real answers to these questions so that you truly *know*.

Real-life example

A courtesy to ensure maximum comprehension. A visit to a predominantly Spanish-speaking school involved a meeting conducted in English with a large group of parents. The majority *spoke* excellent English, and in order to ensure their full comprehension (i.e., understanding beyond the literal) of the conversation, the school principal had ensured the provision of simple headsets and simultaneous interpretation throughout for those who wished to take advantage of this facility. This was a genuinely customer focused and thoughtful decision, revealing the high value that the principal placed upon good communication in her international community. This considerate action was hugely appreciated, and the parents participated fully in the meeting and with full understanding of the information shared.

This practical example shows how communication can be highly effective with careful thought as to the way in which it is shared, strengthening a leader's personal effectiveness and efficiency—and customer relations!

Pause for thought

Now it is time for *you* to make constructive decisions based upon your newfound awareness and reflections.

What do you need to do to improve your communication?

In *Blue Ocean Leadership* by W. Chan Kim and Renee Mauborgne (2015), the authors remind us that whoever a leader is and however laudable their personal traits, the sign of good leadership will be in their actions:

> Focus on acts and activities. Over many years, a great deal of research has generated insights into the values, qualities, and behavioural styles that make for good leadership, and these have formed the basis of development programs and executive coaching. *Blue Ocean Leadership*, by contrast, focuses on what acts and activities leaders need to undertake to boost their teams' motivation and business results, not on who leaders need to be. This difference in emphasis is important. It is markedly easier to change people's acts and activities than their values, qualities, and behavioural traits.

Actions

We have reached the point on our journey where it is time to focus on actions. What do we need to do now? What specific strategies and activities are we going to introduce that will improve our communications significantly? This is particularly critical in an international setting, where the best way to communicate may not fit the traditional and conventional way of sharing information. For example, in some countries, computers and email are not suitable as not all colleagues have access to computers and smartphones and certain types of interactive and social media are rigorously controlled… and Internet access may be intermittent. There are organizations and countries in which physical face-to-face time is considered the courteous "norm." It's critical to understand the most culturally sensitive and effective way to communicate within our organization. Particularly relevant now as virtual and in person are interchangeable.

Contributing to a communications' strategy

Ask yourself, "What do I do that works (and how do I know?)?" and more importantly, "What doesn't work, and why?" Carefully answering these questions will provide starting points for a communication strategy that addresses the issues on as many levels as possible. It may not be the leader's responsibility in an international setting to develop the overall communication strategy. However, as a school leader, you will certainly be expected to contribute honest developmental input to the decision-making behind the final strategy before it is completed. Worth remembering that interim reviews of the strategy will help maintain effectiveness!

You will be well placed to contribute in a number of ways; for example, help the team eliminate insensitive ideas, identify missing information and also who can supply it, comment on feedback that should be taken into account, and also, of course, comment positively on ideas that you believe will improve the communications within your international organization. In situations like this, such leadership attributes as confidence, sensitivity, and integrity will come into their own. It isn't easy as you may be drawing senior colleagues' attention to areas where they think that communications *are* effective while you know, through authentic feedback, that they are not. This may even be a pivotal moment for you when a courageous and sensitive conversation is unavoidable, helping you develop techniques for handling such situations in future.

You may have heard the often-quoted comment, "If you do what you've always done, you'll always get what you've always got" (Henry Ford).

In your organization or team, if you continue to lead in the same way, then you are likely to achieve the same results. These may be quite unsatisfactory to you or your organization's governing body or board. Striving to develop and improve your leadership style will result in heightened personal awareness and a responsiveness that matches the needs of your organization. Effective communication is key.

Communication in an international setting

Getting some basic things right when communicating, both inside and outside your organization, is worth revisiting here as it is such a crucial element toward success. It will mean that instead of frustration and stress, your team members experience a sense of calm and order. Good communications help create better morale, increase output, potentially reduce absenteeism (because people understand their roles and feel motivated), and lead to better staff retention. Staff feel valued, know what they are expected to be doing, and understand the goals and priorities of the organization. Thus, they want to remain part of it, feeling their role is important and their time respected.

New staff may arrive at an international English-speaking school with different levels of English language acquisition and comprehension. Many existing staff will have an excellent command of spoken English that may outstrip the new person's level of understanding, particularly about the use of idioms and colloquial terms. Care is needed then to ensure clarity and avoid ambiguity. Plain, clear, polite language is likely to be best.

A particular minefield is humor, which can be just as treacherous a terrain as religion or politics. It is very important to be aware that the interpretation of what constitutes a humorous comment varies from country to country, even between countries with a language in common. If humor is used at all—and there is a time and a place—it always needs to be contextually and culturally appropriate. Sensitivity is key. If in any doubt in a professional situation, avoid it altogether. If your tone, perhaps intended to be humorous, has been misunderstood, consider very carefully what changes need to be made to the original content or communication style. If it is too late on this occasion, just repair the situation as diplomatically as possible—but learn a lesson for the future.

Humor

As a leader, you will also need to keep an eye (or ear!) on the use of humor within your team. It is essential that you remain alert to colleagues' sensitivities, perhaps revealed through verbal responses to comments by other team members. In these situations, analyze the context before assuming that either party has acted inappropriately. Manage any sensitivities, such as an angry response to a humorous comment which was not the intent. Some colleagues may be disgruntled by being asked to change their style of communicating, particularly the use of humor, because it may offend someone. Some may present a determination to continue in the same vein because "that's who I am, and they can take me or leave me!" Now that both needs addressing and carefully.

It can be quite a challenge for a colleague to sit opposite someone who uses humor habitually and regularly in their communication style. If someone complains to you about a situation like this, ask the person using the humor (in a private one-on-one) to reflect whether their remarks are appropriate. Try and guide them to see the offense they may be causing. This can be with someone from the same cultural background or someone from a different one as humor is not guaranteed to be enjoyed just because you come from the same culture. Encouraging someone to review their personal style is quite daunting and needs that deep breath and courageous approach discussed earlier.

This is when you show your understanding of what makes good communications across cultures, and you demonstrate the strength of character to deal with it. This demonstrates that you are an effective leader with integrity and courage. You are digging deep personally to demonstrate good leadership skills because respect for others is paramount in your working practice. You may feel you would rather not tackle a potentially fractious situation, but your commitment to the diversity within your team or organization should, and indeed must, give you the leverage.

Communicating people's responsibilities

In an international setting, it is more important than ever to be clear and careful in how you communicate people's roles and responsibilities. You will need to ensure that each member of staff:

- Has an individual role description that succinctly sets out their responsibilities
- Has read their role description and discussed it with their line manager
- Knows and understands the role of the team and their role within it
- Know the targets they are working toward (make sure the targets are appropriate, have an achievable timescale, and that the person has access to the resource to help them achieve it).

If you asked your international staff how knowledgeable they feel about the vision and mission of the institution and their interpretation of it, what would they say? How would they answer the question "How do you know what is going on, and how involved do you feel in determining the improvements needed to make it even better?"

Pause for thought

Your success in becoming an inspirational and effective leader will depend, to a very large extent, on your interpersonal and communication skills. Your aim is to develop as a forward-thinking, effective, motivational leader in any setting.

The activities and real-life situations presented below are here to support your reflection time as you work toward this. In each case, ask the following questions:

- How would *you* deal with this?
- What decisions would *you* make? Why?
- How will you check out whether *your* decisions are good ones?
- How can you be sure that your actions are respectful of the cultural diversity within team and community?

Real-life example

The essential qualities of respect and courtesy. An experienced educational leader was invited by a former colleague, a delightful and exceptionally courteous leader, to accompany a newly appointed chief executive officer (CEO) on a visit to one of their schools. The purpose was to provide support with some badly needed development work to improve the school's functionality. A meeting was quickly arranged, and the CEO was charming with many ideas about how he saw the help being delivered. His parting comment was "I shall be in touch." So far, he had demonstrated excellent communication skills: warmth, good body language, smiles, interest.

Then weeks passed; absolutely nothing!

The person who had been approached decided to drop the CEO a line, saying, "I am still here should you need me."

A few days later, she received a friendly "holding" reply, but then again, things went quiet. Clearly, she was of no tactical importance to this new international appointee who certainly had no grasp of the expertise she could offer. The most shocking aspect of this was the lack of courtesy. A simple "At this time, unfortunately, I don't think there is anything we need that would match with your skill set," or words to that effect would have been appropriate. Instead, nothing was communicated.

This showed incredibly poor situational awareness and leadership and demonstrated how the CEO's behaviors toward those he perceived as being of no importance were likely to manifest themselves in his day-to-day working.

The new CEO seemed not to care—or, to give him the benefit of the doubt (always a good leadership trait), was blissfully unaware that his behavior could be perceived as rude.

This person did not appear to see the need for courtesy in saying "no" to someone, perhaps seeing the situation as "just business procedure." If he was genuinely and completely unaware of how rude and unprofessional this behavior appeared, this also was failing. Perhaps his communication was brilliant "upward," i.e., to people senior to him, but sadly his actions (or lack of appropriate action) made it clear that he saw no value in proffering similarly good and courteous communication to those perceived to be "below" him.

Actions that impact a professional profile

The type of behavior in this example is detrimental to a person's professional profile and significantly damages the external reputation of their organization. The international world is a remarkably small one in terms of professional reputation in a specific field and provides a very effective grapevine for bad experiences.

In international school settings, a leader who manages upward only can prove to be a difficult colleague to work with or be led by, as we saw in chapter 3. Such people tend to respond only to the head office senior personnel or most senior colleague, perceiving that only this person can help them in their career. They do not see the value of spending time with grassroots colleagues, understanding or responding to issues in order to improve communications on the ground. This can make for a very tense and frustrating environment with staff often feeling that there is no one to whom they can turn in order to discuss problems as this leader sees them as unimportant and is simply not interested in them or their issues at all.

You may be familiar with the phrase: "Be nice to people on your way up because you'll meet them on your way down" (Wilson Mizner). This is indeed a salutary lesson and a sobering thought for all leaders.

The skill of saying more by saying less

We have looked in earlier chapters at the ability of great leaders to listen. *Truly* listening also means taking on board what is being said and acting upon it when appropriate. Great leaders also perceive and understand the more subtle messages delivered by facial expression and body language and may have an intuition about what is left unsaid. A great leader of an international school has undertaken some due diligence on the intercultural mix and recent institutional heritage of the staff, including newly appointed members. These leaders demonstrate valuing their staff and send a signal that says, "I am looking forward to working with you."

Communicating in ways other than words

Is it just the words you say that make a good impression? Well, no: clearly, it is also your manner and demeanor. Body language is an interesting and important dimension of communication, and good eye contact (in a culture where this is acceptable; however, in some regions of Asia and Africa, this is inappropriate).

Facial expressions that show engagement, nodding periodically to demonstrate that you are on board and are listening, and culturally appropriate hand gestures are incredibly helpful tools in building empathy. Regarding hand gestures, it is well worth the work to research generally acceptable forms of hand gestures in the culture where you are working as you could easily give offense unintentionally. A simple hand gesture that is normal in one culture can be highly offensive in another. Note that the modern international economy has given rise to some changes in culturally acceptable body language and gestures, so when doing your research, be sure to use up-to-date sources.

Overall, try to relax. Be authentic and avoid overthinking it as this could lead to self-conscious "stances" that may appear odd and undermine the sense of trust you seek to build. The key is simplicity. The balance between your natural physical demeanor and any deliberate adjustments you make to your movements or positioning should be a subtle one. In the greatest leaders, changes eventually become subconscious and natural, an authentic part of who *you* are.

Learning to interact subtly while listening

While listening, it is often appropriate to give occasional verbal signs of encouragement in a supportive tone: for example, "Uh-huh, yes, of course, I agree." Make sure any follow-up comment you make is well timed and elicits more information. Why is this important? Well, if you were to remain silent throughout, your colleague might dry up, feeling anxious about what they were trying to say, or might feel either that they were going on too long or that you, the listener, had lost interest. Intermittent verbal responses help ensure this doesn't happen.

There are cultural considerations here too, and one may be your own. Some people have been trained to take a straight, to-the-point approach since an early age whilst others feel more at home, enjoying the story. Good leaders know their team, and themselves, and can adjust the character of the conversation accordingly.

Remember, too, that some verbal responses will be interpreted as encouragement so only use these when that is your intent. For example, if a staff member is sharing hostile feelings about a colleague, you will want to get to the bottom of the matter without fueling any animosity between the two individuals. It important not to make a judgment here or offer advice. Your action is listening—actively!

Giving reassurance

It may be appropriate to restate what someone has said in order to check for understanding or accuracy. This is a reassuring sign for the speaker that that you are focused on what they are saying and working to understand it. Such reassurance also gives the speaker an opportunity to divulge more information. Indications of "I value what you are saying" are strong and purposeful. In confidential situations or where a colleague has drawn on their own courage to bring an issue to your attention, reassurance will give them the confidence to go on.

Skillful questioning

Be careful and thoughtful about the types of questions you use for different purposes.

- *Open* questions give the speaker the opportunity to share their ideas, suggestions, or concerns.
- *Probing* questions help you understand more clearly the ideas or issues raised (though they must be framed and delivered sensitively).
- *Factual* questions, or closed questions, have limited use when you are listening to someone's concerns as they can limit and close off what the person wants to say; however, such questions may be useful: for example, if the person makes an allegation of bullying, you might need to ask, "Who said that to you?" or "When did this occur?" or something similar.

Skillful, relevant questioning is achievable when you have been listening acutely and therefore understand the best way to help the colleague further explain the situation. Questioning appropriately will help the person express their feelings on the issue more clearly or calmly. This isn't about having a checklist of, say, ten must-ask questions that you will systematically go through—that could make the discussion appear to be an interview or an interrogation. Instead, it is about pulling from your leadership skill set the right question for the right occasion. Your aim must always be to instill confidence in the person you are speaking with, enabling them to set out the issue clearly. This can be achieved by asking the right type of question.

Demonstrating empathy

Empathy and reflecting back what you hear can be very effective in delicate one-on-one conversations, demonstrating to the speaker that you understand their feelings. Your comments should acknowledge what is being expressed.

Many of us have been in a situation where this did not happen. We needed empathy from the person listening, and they offered none whatsoever, making us feel worse. For example, a person who has taken some annual leave to recover from several stressful and personally upsetting weeks does not want to get a call from their manager along the lines of "I realize you are on vacation after a fraught time. However, I need this piece of work by tomorrow. Sorry to disturb and all that, is there a possibility that you might be able to do it?" Here, the speaker is feigning empathy ("I realize…") and yet is putting additional pressure on the person.

Some people believe that empathy is an innate characteristic; you are either empathetic or not—while others believe, correctly, that it can be learned. Empathy is about knowing when people need to hear or see you demonstrate some form of understanding and then doing so. This knowledge can be gained by attentive watching and listening. Being empathetic isn't about agreeing with everything someone says but about indicating that you understand what they are going through. Don't make it about you; for example, "I understand completely. Last year, my dog died, and I was so upset too," and if you say you understand, be sure that you do as false empathy is worse than ignorance.

Empathy is about finding words and body language that offer subliminal, gentle support or understanding; for example, "I am so sorry to hear that. I can't imagine how upsetting this must be for you." It is also about helping move the conversation on; for example, "Is there anything that would help right now? Would you like to take some time off this afternoon?"

Reflecting on someone's words to consolidate understanding

The use of the phrase "I wonder..." can be incredibly helpful in both clarifying what has been said and in offering an alternative view of the immediate issue without appearing judgmental; for example, "I wonder how you feel about that action?" or "I wonder what might happen if you..."

Helping someone reflect on their own approach, actions, and behaviors, or how they feel about something that happened to them is to provide them with powerful tool that may help them sort out the issue themselves by a process of reflecting or "thinking aloud." If you can lead a person into this mindset, the conversation may turn with the person now articulating their own solution to the problem and asking you, the listener, what you think of their plan. This is a great outcome. Make sure, though, that you provide any support they might need to take things forward.

Less experienced colleagues may respond particularly well to the "I wonder" questions. Perhaps it is the first time they have embarked on the journey of reflection that, all being well, will become habitual, strengthening them and developing their confidence on their own path toward leadership.

This and indeed all the approaches and actions outlined above are ways of building a rapport with an individual and demonstrating you are engaged with them and what they have to say. The value of these approaches cannot be underestimated.

Communicating well in meetings to ensure success

What are the best strategies for efficient, time-saving communication in relation to meetings? Here are four simple tips. Ensure that you:

- Know that the meeting is necessary
- Identify the actions you want to take
- Plan ahead
- Come prepared.

Looking at this with a bit more detail, there are three stages: before the meeting, during the meeting, and after the meeting.

Before the meeting. Communicate clearly and carefully about the expectations you have from the meeting and how long you expect it to take. Stick to that timing. You should:

- Set purposeful agendas and send them out twenty-four hours in advance to give everyone a chance to prepare
- Use a form of communication that is right for your international setting, ensuring that it is accessible for those colleagues who do not have email or the language skills to read English.

During the meeting. A meeting is all about communication as a means of achieving something. To ensure this happens effectively, you should:

- Come to a meeting well prepared with any necessary materials at hand
- Revisit the goals and keep focused on them as you chair the meeting
- Stick to the agenda and timings, ensuring someone takes minutes or notes
- Let everyone have a say but keep them to the point and do not let them ramble
- Keep to the planned length of the meeting to promote focus and action, rather than letting the discussion drift on aimlessly
- Agree on the decision taken and follow-up actions needed and ensure that these are noted down.

After the meeting. A meeting is only successful if it sets in motion certain desired outcomes and decisions that arise from it. You should:

- Have reliable ways of checking that each meeting has been effective, decisions are acted on (with the key being the

documentation and rapid sharing of concise and including succinct accurate action points), and everyone's time is well spent (think about what communication methods you would use to achieve this)
- Check with the team as to whether they see the meetings as effective and efficient (do they have ideas for improvement?)
- Decide what types of communication will help you know whether the team is on track with the agreed actions
- Share the notes from the meeting swiftly so that people know what they are expected to do next (think about how you should share the information if not everyone is completely confident in spoken and written English)
- Evaluate the effectiveness of your communications policy for those who do not have email or the language skills to read English—how do you ensure that this is updated and relevant considering the frequently changing teams that tend to be a feature of international schools?

Pause for thought

Once you have identified your actual practice as a result of reflection and feedback, you are able to identify a few simple actions that will have the maximum impact in helping you improve it. Promise yourself what you are going to do to be more effective, setting aside time in your weekly plan to work on these actions. The sense of satisfaction and achievement will be great at the end of the week as you will have covered more than you thought possible and will feel more in control of your work rate and output. You may also be pleasantly surprised when an employee survey reflects good communications on behalf of the school.

Real-life example

A relaxed opportunity to review success. An experienced leader would always bring her leadership team together at the end of Friday from 4:00 p.m. to 4:30 p.m. with an end-of-the-week treat (usually chocolate or appropriate edibles to ensure inclusivity—even treats can be tricky given people's dietary choices!) to identify what had been achieved that week. The senior team would spend this time reflecting on the successes and what is still left to do.

The leader had determined that the treat would not be perceived as a patronizing softener, even positive gestures can be misinterpreted unless the purpose is made clear by her choice of words. The team would make a list of successes on the whiteboard and take the time to recognize the people who had helped them get there. There was always an element of surprise that so much *had* been achieved as schools are very apt to quickly gloss over successes, always looking out for what needs to be done next.

The leader would then make sure that the communication sent out to parents at the end of each week thanked the staff specifically by outlining what they had achieved and how the students had benefitted. This was invaluable as there was tremendous pressure to make big changes and achieve significantly better outcomes swiftly. It would have been all too easy to catapult from one activity to another, demanding that staff focus on a succession of different things with unrealistically short timelines, leading to burnout and frustration. Instead, giving credit where due helped bring a demoralized staff alongside as they worked together to effect rapid improvements. At the end of each week, the team had a sense of authentic achievement.

Escaping the dead hand of digital media

The growing number of instant electronic methods of written communication—email, texts, and probably even newer methods—by the time this book reaches you is both alarming and frustrating. Time spent reading or answering unnecessary messages distracts you from the job you should be doing, reduces productivity, and can cause significant stress. There is also the "danger zone" of the immediacy with which such communications can be received. Responding in haste, anger, or without considering the audience has been the downfall of people in many different walks of life. A useful rule of thumb is to set up a reply but then walk away and reconsider before sending. The view of a trusted colleague playing the part of the intended recipient (if confidentiality is not compromised) can be helpful. Also, the various translation facilities—incredibly useful as they may be—are not always as accurate as we would like; a genuinely well-thought-out message may fall foul of an inanimate translator. To avoid this pitfall, write your original message in plain, polite, idiom-free language with short sentences and avoid humor.

Real-life example

Frustration-free Friday. In one discussion with a school team on the pressures of electronic communication, there were numerous comments about how many messages staff were receiving, particularly from parents, and how frustrated and pressured they felt. It appeared that this was really impacting morale and draining energy.

So the staff agreed on a strategy. There was to be a "No Email Day" every Friday (for most organizations, this works well as the last day of the week). This decision was shared with parents, giving clear reasons and clarifying that phone calls from parents would be answered promptly (in case there was an emergency or a key concern) but that staff would not be opening or responding to emails on Fridays.

Parents had mixed views on this, but most respected the valid reasons behind the request. Staff really found it helpful. Even so, they had to train themselves not to write emails on a Thursday/Friday (depending on location) ready to press send on Saturday/Sunday or Monday! The policy succeeded in reducing the time-wasting email culture significantly. There was a perception that people were managing their time better and getting into the habit of resolving matters face-to-face before they became an issue.

As part of this strategy, staff were asked to apply the following test to decide whether an email was necessary.

In the absence of digital communication channels, would they create a note in longhand on the issue?

If they would, then they should send the email. If not, then the matter was not important enough to be put in writing: the email should not be sent. Instead, the matter should be resolved by speaking directly either on the phone or in person.

Reducing the burden of constant communication

Reducing the burden of electronic communication needs a simple cultural shift—informed by how things were done before the digital revolution. If someone is in the same building, or indeed just across the room, we all know that the tried-and-tested method is to *go and see the person and talk*. Nothing ever replaces face-to-face communication where this is physically and logistically possible.

A change like the one in the example is not just about agreeing on a policy that you think will be effective. It is about acting on it, sticking to it, and giving it a chance to work. In this case, the policy freed up valuable time and brought about a change of atmosphere, one that was much more relaxed and productive. Could you consider something similar within your team? How would it be agreed upon, explained, and phased in?

Self-discipline with smartphones and other gadgets in the workplace

Is it necessary to include a subsection on this topic? Sadly, yes. By now, many of us have been in meetings where at least one person has kept their phone at hand with alerts activated and has read a message, sent a message, or answered a call, often when the team is in the middle of a key discussion. The subliminal message from that person is, *You and your ideas are less important than this.*

Real-life example

A quorum but with no one really present. At one weekly board meeting in a company where there was no "step away from the phone" protocol, there were twelve people present in the room, eleven of whom used their phone at some point during the meeting—with at least two people leaving the room to take a call.

This is an example of where communications were poor. The nonverbal message being conveyed was that everyone in the room took second place to the incoming communications on the handheld devices.

The message that each of those eleven people conveyed to their colleagues was: *Whatever else is happening in my life, it is more important than what I am doing in this meeting with this group of people.* There is also a somewhat arrogant implication: *I am so important that I need to be constantly available at any time and nothing can happen without my input.*

These are not the impressions that you want to give. If they are, your presence at the meeting would in any case be a waste of time as well as a distraction.

Digital devices

Digital devices have become so attached to us—or us to them—that some people feel they must always respond to them. This devotion to an inanimate object is disrespectful to the people around you and can be detrimental to an organization. If we do not set out expectations of courtesy on this matter, as a protocol, then many people will not understand or be aware of others' feelings and how disrespectful they find this behavior to be. We must be courageous, discuss the issue, and agree on protocols for meetings; then we must hold people to account. This is particularly key in international schools as some teachers have arrived from countries, or institutional cultures, where this devotion to devices is not only acceptable but the norm.

Great leaders do not behave with their staff or colleagues in any way that belittles them or pointedly shows that they are not important. Everyone is important to great leaders. You can, and should, make meetings a "no phone zone" or "no ping wing." There is very little in the business world that cannot wait for up to sixty minutes while business conversations are happening. If there is something perceived to be critical on the horizon, then an explanation and an apology at the beginning of the meeting is required. Your team should know why the phone is on. This may be a hard rule to implement consistently as people have become so dependent on this form of communication and can feel "lost" or "anxious" without it, but that does not mean they can't survive without it for an hour at least.

Every organization should have a phone and text policy that all members are involved in creating. It needs to be concise and factual, outlining when a digital device may, and may not, be in use and (just as importantly) why.

Pause for thought

It is time to check up on your own attitudes to digital devices. See how you fare with the following questions:

- What are your personal actions in relation to electronic communication when in meetings with others? Do you keep your phone on and check or answer messages, and if so, ask yourself why?
- How often do you use the phone or answer texts when you are in conversation with someone, often saying "Oh, sorry, I have to take this"?
- How often (hopefully never!) do you read/listen to a message when someone in the same room is talking to you?

None of the above actions demonstrates good communication, social skills, or leadership. Instead, they convey a negative leadership message. If you think you are guilty of any of the above habits, it is time to determinedly stamp them out.

The benefits versus the potential cruelty of social media

The birth and proliferation of social media has created a new dilemma for leaders. Businesses can and do flourish by dint of the skillful and appropriate use of social media when its possibilities are harnessed in a positive way. However, these platforms can also turn an organization into a threatening place to work if colleagues use any of the plethora of constantly evolving social media platforms to discuss internal issues inappropriately outside the workplace or to complain about, ridicule, or belittle a colleague. Owing to the vagaries of social media (who's a "friend" of who, who can post on whose timeline), hateful comments can also be posted without the victims having the opportunity to reply or defend themselves.

If online breaches of confidentiality or bullying come to light, then there is no alternative but to remove this person from the team. We have all read of situations where comments, intentionally hurtful or otherwise, have led to deep distress and sometimes, in extreme cases, long-term mental illness or suicide. Great leaders ensure that all members of their team or organization know that there is a "No Tolerance Policy" around cyberbullying. This is an important communication to get right in to in order to prevent situations that could cause distress or harm. On the rare occasions that this does happen, then the colleague must understand the critical human resource steps that will need to be taken by the organization as a result.

Successful leaders have a concise social media policy in place that is shared with all colleagues, who must sign to say they have read it and will adhere to it. Its essence should be that when using social media, staff are *not* permitted to:

- Share confidential information
- Intimidate, bully, or stalk a colleague
- Post comments, good or bad, about the team or the organization's work or personnel.

The successful leader makes clear their expectation that the team will be known internally and externally for its professional and respectful stance in all forms of communication.

All this should be, quite simply, nonnegotiable. A strong clear message from a leader and the leader's commitment to this shows a genuine belief in and commitment to valuing and respecting staff and providing a safe and secure environment in which to work.

Before we leave the topic of social media, it is also worth noting that many potential employers will access candidates' social media sites independently as part of the interview process. There have been instances where a new role has been lost before the interview stage because the content of the candidate's social media feeds suggested they would not be a suitable person to employ. It hardly needs saying that a leader's own practice in this regard should be beyond reproach, both to set an example to colleagues and for the sake of their future career.

Face-to-face conversations

"I know that you believe what you think I said, but I'm not sure you realize that what you heard is not what I meant" (Robert McCloskey, Pentagon spokesman, during a press briefing on the Vietnam War).

Some conversations and nonverbal communications that we are involved in make us feel good. We feel we have listened well, shared information in a good way, and that everything is moving along as we would wish. Everyone involved in the conversation is feeling good about it. For example, when a performance review is full of positives and you can say or hear, "Congratulations, you are really doing well in this role because you…," then everyone leaves with the feel-good factor. Incidentally, it's important to reiterate exactly *what* is creating the success!

Alternatively, some conversations do not go well at all, e.g., perhaps someone reacted badly to guidance they were being given, or the leader had a bad day and did not express themselves with as much diplomacy as they intended. If you have had a conversation which you felt did not go well, the best way to make the situation positive is to reflect on what went wrong and what you can learn from it. If, later in the day or week, you pass the person you had been talking to in a corridor or elsewhere, the best approach is a simple smile, asking, "Would it be possible for us to catch up at the end of the day?" This doesn't feel threatening or worrisome. If the same words are said with a frown and the tone is curt, then you set a very different set of expectations, but the simple friendly approach will give the person hope that things are going to be resolved—and in a calm, kind, and reassuring manner.

Some conversations become indicators of the kind of people that we should avoid becoming in both our professional and our personal lives. Many of us have had the experience of being in a conversation with someone who seems very attentive and engaged in what we are discussing until another person whom they consider to be more important, useful, or influential appears in the vicinity. Then the apparent "connection" is lost as our partner in dialogue loses the thread and abruptly ends the conversation to pursue another one they perceive as more beneficial.

Before we leave the crucial subject of communications, it is worth recommending the following book by [8]Daniel Goleman: *Focus: The Hidden Driver of Excellence.* In it, Goleman draws our attention to communications and the importance of leaders focusing on the wider world: "Leaders with a strong outward focus," he says, "are not only good listeners but also good questioners."

Pause for thought

This is the ideal time to reflect on the substance of this chapter. There is a great deal to consider here and to add to your self-analysis and personal action plan. As you complete work on your self-analysis about communication skills, a good question to ask and answer as a starting point is, "Were there any surprises?"

The power of 3

Three quotations:

> Many can argue—not many converse. (Amos Bronson Alcott [1799–1888], American teacher, writer, and philosopher)

---

[8] Daniel Goleman, *Focus: The Hidden Driver of Excellence* (Harper, 2013).

A businessman's conversation should be regulated by fewer and simpler rules than any other function of the human animal. They are: have something to say, say it, stop talking. (Our favorite and most underused piece of advice!) (George Horace Lorimer [1899–1937], American editor of the *Saturday Evening Post*)

The first ingredient in conversation is truth, the next good sense, the third, good humour, and the fourth, wit. (Sir William Temple [1555–1627], English baronet, statesman, and essayist)

Three books to challenge your thinking further:

- Noor Al-Deen, Hana S. (editor), and John Allen Hendricks (editor). *Social Media and Strategic Communications.* Hampshire, UK, 2013.
- Dixon, Dale. *Sweating Bullets: A Story about Overcoming the Fear of Public Speaking.* Eagle, Idaho, 2014.
- Porterfield, Kitty, and Meg Carnes. *Why Social Media Matters: School Communication in the Digital Age.* Bloomington, Indiana, 2004.

CHAPTER 7

Now Is Exactly the Right Time

We are moving away from reflections on leadership behaviors, dispositions, and strategies to actions. These form a professional tool kit to use when the time is right. It is worth remembering that actions are never taken in isolation. They merge with other strategies too, and there is always feedback.

We are looking at actions one at a time, focusing on their purpose and benefits. These are actions that a leader may take at a particular time to help others and increase their effectiveness. This kind of support may also meet the leader's personal professional needs at a specific point in their career. Judging when to employ the right actions is the skill.

Doug Sundheim in his book, [9]*Taking Smart Risks*, shares the view about simplified thinking around leadership and what makes a good leader. He is urging a move away from clichés:

> In fifteen minutes and six brief lines, I captured my current thinking about great leadership exactly as it came to me. Here's what came out.

---

[9] Doug Sundheim, *Taking Smart Risks: How Sharp Leaders Win When Stakes are High* (New York: Gildan Media LLC, 2013).

"I believe…

1) There's too much noise in business today.
2) Playing it safe is dangerous.
3) Mediocrity is cancerous. Once you begin to accept mediocrity, it sends signals that it's acceptable.
4) Unless you're relentlessly open and honest in your communication—constantly—things fall apart.
5) Great leaders create the conditions for other people's greatness to come out.
6) You need to hold people's feet to the fire. Do it with respect. But don't let people off the hook.

Simple, clear, authentic actions.

Coaching for improvement

Being a good coach as a leader isn't a given. Some leaders are natural; others do not find it easy as there can be a tremendous temptation to say, "If I was you, I would…"

Effective coaching can bring success as it is a structured way of working collaboratively with someone to help them. Attuned coaches understand that there is a continuum between coaching and mentoring and that finding the sweet spot, on that continuum, is critical. Coaching can help establish, at the beginning, what the colleague believes they are good at. Healthy debate and discussions can then occur over planned times to help identify what needs to be improved. Establishing what the actual expected improvement will be at the beginning and the actions with defined success criteria can provide impetus for the person being coached—a sense of excitement for the journey ahead.

There are various coaching models to choose from, so it is important to identify one that isn't too formulaic. One that allows the coach and colleague to choose the right direction with each conversation. Any mechanism for reflecting on practice and looking at ways to improve with an experienced and successful partner is a profitable one, especially in an international setting. There are often fewer opportunities to attend professional learning conferences or work with local experts. Successful coaching doesn't just happen, so careful planning and the right approach for the person partnering this is what is needed before any conversations begin.

Coaching a colleague can build trust, but the significant challenge here is to ensure there is no slip into a personal relationship. Keep the coaching/partner relationship professional. To verge into friendship with coaching sessions simply being meetings with continuous platitudes isn't good for anyone. Maintain the invisible barrier. Be thoughtful, be an active listener, seek clarity, discuss wisely and empathetically, and employ some rigor where and when appropriate. The coaching relationship is then effective as it both challenges practice while motivating leadership growth.

There is also a cultural aspect to this partnership. The leader may consider that they are the best person for the role of coach and may outwardly be accepted positively by the colleague wanting a coach. Remember that some team members may view the leadership from a respected stance and may be unwilling or unable to be as open in the coaching session as they may be with a less senior colleague. Previous organizational experiences and personal cultural behaviors may be additional barriers that need work to resolve. Be alert to the body language and conversational language when the choice of coach is discussed. What *is* the message?

A leader's coaching should involve a variety of tailored activities sharply targeted to enhance improvement. This partnership approach requires the leader/coach to be:

1) *Sensitive* to the colleague and clear about what they will be doing and why
2) *Open and honest* with the issues laid out clearly to ensure understanding
3) *Build trust* by setting out areas for development and how progress will be evaluated

4) *Setting the work* in context as it must be relevant to the situation and understood by the partner; strategies and actions are fit for purpose.

5) *Responsive* to culture practices demonstrating you have researched the colleague thoughtfully and are cognizant to their needs, e.g., not booking sessions on a Friday if the partner's culture has Friday as a holy day.

6) *Observe, analyze,* and *reflect* with the partner on what is occurring during the coaching:
   - What is the specific aim?
   - What is the body language like at the beginning?
   - Are the sessions effective in your eyes?
   - How much dialogue comes from the partner?
   - What progress is being made?
   - What is not working?
   - What can be changed?
   - What *is* working effectively and how can this be built upon?

A coach should continuously be encouraging the colleague to reflect and honestly evaluate the approach they have taken and, most importantly, its impact. Good coaches resist the temptation to tell their partner what to do. They focus instead on highlighting choices that still empowers the partner to take control and make their own decisions.

A thoughtful leader/coach helps the new aspirant leader to reflect on the big picture, their actions, team responses, desired outcomes, and actual ones. The coach becomes the mirror. All successful leaders possess the ability to be reflectively self-aware, and they know and understand that bringing the team along with them, collaborating on the appropriate big decisions, leads to a focused, successful, and proactive team.

An awkward challenge

The leader may not be the right choice of coach for certain members of the team, and just because the leader wants to be a leader who coaches, it does not always mean that the leader's interpersonal skills and style is the right match. Never be afraid to make the change of coach if the partnership is not working. It is equally important not to take offense if someone approaches the coach and says, "This isn't working for me."

Be sure to respond by saying, "Then let's discuss what *would* work for you, and we can make that happen."

It is important also to be clear that the courageous action of requesting a change is a mature action and is to be celebrated.

In this way, the leader is modeling for the person seeking support that:

a. The leader wants to ensure the support is right for the partner
b. The leader is also working on their own learning too as there are things they can/could do better.

This way of operating conveys a very strong message of a reflective leader focused on getting it right for a colleague—a leadership ego that doesn't get in the way. This way of working also enables a leader to show empathy, reading the signs of how compatible a coach they are. Hearing difficult messages takes courage. Great leaders have courage!

Real-life example

A colleague is not a natural lover of gym workouts. Recently, she decided she needed to do something about her level of fitness and reluctantly yet determinedly went to a fitness club to sign in. This colleague knew she needed a personal trainer (coach) or else she simply wouldn't go. She was assigned a delightful trainer/coach. The colleague started out by being very clear about what she felt she could do, couldn't do, and wouldn't do! The coach was *very* skillful. She worked out that the "bullish" stance was based on nervousness and took things very slowly with the colleague, explaining all the time what she was doing and why.

The colleague had great difficulty completing any kind of circuit in the beginning and could only manage eight repetitions of the most basic exercises. Rather than have her leave deflated, the coach drew her attention to things like considered body positioning and how this was benefitting her work and the effort she was putting in. Over time the colleague noticed the change in her own approach; when the coach would say, "Let's do eight push-ups," the colleague would say, "I think I could do ten"—ownership of the process and empowerment emerging from a simple yet highly effective coaching technique.

There was never a time when the coach suggested that she had done anything wrong. Instead, the coach would stop and explain what our colleague could do to improve her output further. She structured the plan daily and enabled the colleague to focus on the activities she liked to begin with and then introduced new task after new task. The colleague found that she was discussing small achievements and began to take much more care on her eating habits and increased her water-drinking regime too. The coach had, with sensitive and very skillful handling, changed *actions* to improve skills and fitness levels. At no time did the coach subscribe to the colleague's "I can't do this" mantra and turned it around to a much more positive "I can do this" one.

The coach took considerable time to understand an approach and style and, so importantly, respected the fear.

Lessons learned from being a coach can be filed in a leader's mental action box for reference. We all need to pull ideas from this box occasionally. We *all* need to listen to critical friends at some time!

A leader listening and hearing

The skill of recognizing and valuing silence is an unusual one and possibly one that many leaders believe they demonstrate daily. An empathetic and skilled leader uses body language and affirming words when appropriate to help the aspiring leader reach the decision or answer. We know it is critical that the leader/coach does not *provide* the answer and teases out the thinking until a decision is reached.

Moving confidently toward independence

Leadership coaches whose aim is to help their colleagues become independent and confident leaders are motivational. This success should be the aim of all leaders; to help the trainee be a professional, successful learner, they are able to:

- Respond proactively to advice and analysis
- Understand their own learning leadership needs and strengths
- Take a greater role in deciding their actions
- Take a greater role in testing out their theories with the leader/coach first
- Be painfully honest in their self-review and amend appropriately and *swiftly*
- Take risks on occasions.

Modeling

Modeling behavior is frequently identified as an important action for leaders. There is a need to be very specific as to how you go about it. First, leaders need to be clear about what behaviors they *need* to model! This requires the same amount of thought and structure as all the other leadership strategies.

Simply smiling and saying good morning to everyone each day because you want this to be the practice in your organization does not necessarily mean it will happen and everyone will do it. Within any organization, there will be attentive people who see the leader's behavior and understand the expectation of modeling it. There will be those who simply do not see it and will need a different approach to make the changes, and there will be those who see it but have absolutely no intention of doing it.

Be an influencer

To influence cultural change effectively, leaders need to open the discussion with all staff to understand present behaviors—what we do and why and then open a frank discussion about what needs to be better. It is incredibly important to understand whether colleagues consider that the changes you are proposing are important too.

If the changes that the leader wishes to see are important and yet consultation with colleagues tells them that they do not have the same view, then the way in which the leader sets the scene for change will be challenging. It will require high-level communication skills aligned with sensitivity to the organization's history.

This doesn't mean that a leader doesn't do it, but it may simply be worth taking a little longer in thinking through the how.

A leader may decide to align themselves with a small number of colleagues who agree with the change strategy in the hope this may help the change along. Caution is urged, though, as developing a them and us is *not* the desired outcome. There would be no positive outcomes.

At times, there may be certain behaviors you want to see in place that no one else has mentioned or sees as important, for example, in an office setting, a clear desk policy whether literal or figurative at the end of each day. The leader may feel that this is nonnegotiable; therefore, sharing this expectation and explaining why it is important will enable colleagues to model it, experiencing success.

A point to note: It isn't enough to assume it will happen continuously. Reminding people quietly and respectfully when the practice is not as expected is important. Colleagues need to see this expected behavior as forming part of the culture of the organization. Good leaders never call people out publicly. They do so quietly and respectfully through a one-on-one conversation.

Regular reviews of modeling behavior

It is often good to review with the team and self-review also how each person behaves during a week or month. Just spend an hour checking out if the behaviors agreed are happening and what the impact has been. Ticking off positives really does build the culture of pride and commitment. Everyone can experience the feel-good factor. People's efforts are being realized, and they can see the difference they are making. This pause for reflection can also help catch something that may have fallen by the wayside or is only being modeled by a few people on the team rather than the whole.

Doug Sundheim says: "Do not settle for mediocrity but model great behaviors *at all times*."

Leave the audience wanting more!

When a leader coaches a larger group such as in-person training sessions, they must be seen accessible to all colleagues. Making themselves available to the staff afterward is a thoughtful way to recognize that some colleagues do not have the confidence to ask questions in large meetings. Being seen as approachable and available to all whilst protecting some time for themselves shows the value placed on respecting everyone's views. This models best practice.

Even if someone is combative or angry about what is being asked and wants to take the leader to task, *listen* first, maintain eye contact (if culturally acceptable), and then consider how best to diffuse the situation. At the same time, truly hear what could be beneficial for improvement. Sometimes an offer to meet later in a one-on-one situation is a significant win. Defusing a public spat is the priority but listening to hear is the second.

Leadership rehearsals

Success that looks easy only comes with rehearsal. The actions we need to take any time we are speaking to large audiences (and how large is likely to be based on experience and confidence) are:

- Prepare thoroughly
- Practice, practice, practice

- Support tools should be simple and aiding the delivery does not detract from it
- Make eye contact (as appropriate), smile
- Conclude with a short review, smile, and engage one-on-one afterward where possible.

Pause for reflection

This chapter shows us how we can do it! It is worth remembering that it isn't acquiring one skill that makes a great leader; it is skillfully managing a compendium, great communication, collegiality, honesty, confidence, resilience, collaboration. *All* come in to play. Great leaders care about their people and want them to succeed, celebrate when they do, and inspire them to even greater heights.

The power of 3

Three quotations to ponder:

> Behavior is the mirror in which everyone shows their image. (Johann Wolfgang von Goethe, German playwright and poet, [1749–1832])

> The single biggest problem in communication is the illusion that it has taken place. (George Bernard Shaw, Irish playwright and co-founder of the London School of Economics [1856–1950])

> Do what you can, with what you've got, where you are. (Theodore Roosevelt, Twenty-Sixth President of the United States)

Three books to challenge your thinking further:

- Barsh, Joanna, and Johanne Lavoie. *Centered Leadership: A Field Guide for Leading with Positive Impact and Resilience.* New York, 2014.
- Howell, Jon P., and Dan L. Costley. *Understanding Behaviors for Effective Leadership,* 2nd edition. London, 2005.
- Kahneman, Daniel. *Noise: A Flaw in Human Judgment.* Little, Brown, Spark, May 2021.

CHAPTER 8

Yes, We Can Be Both

We have spent time exploring and trialing simple actions that improve day-to-day leadership effectiveness. We have taken a deep look at the resultant effectiveness of a team that we either lead or belong to. Now it is time to revisit and challenge our *personal* attitude and behaviors considering what we have learned. One last time! Trustworthy *and* authentic. How can you be *both*?

Having researched the behaviors and characteristics exemplified by great leaders in the earlier chapters, we focused on great attitudes, behaviors, and actions. Effective leaders know when and how to motivate individual people, teams, and organizations. This prework now helps us take a deep dive into ourselves. Really good leaders take the time to identify what they are proud of and what they now want to do better.

Not perfect?

Just stop and recognize that no one is perfect. Be true to yourself as you peel away the onion layers of your leadership attitudes, behaviors, and competencies. Know what you *can* manage at this time. Identify what you want to challenge yourself with. You know not to jump to do everything straight away. It is simply not possible. Time for reflection is never wasted, and the *right* time is *your* time.

Reflecting in an international setting

In an international organization where each person brings their own cultural experiences to the team, it is important to remember that these aspects impact directly on our perception of ourselves and others: "We are the sum of all people we have ever met; you change the tribe, and the tribe changes you" (@Dirk Wittenborn).

Dive right in

We are now diving deep into the most difficult of issues that provides evidence of honesty and integrity. It is *so* much easier to describe times when someone has been dishonest and shown a lack of integrity. There just isn't a checklist to tick and confirm that this is you. Only *you* know if these are words you can use truthfully to describe yourself.

The following questions are here to challenge. A basic yes or no is required, not a long-drawn-out explanation of why you think so. The responses here are just for you. Long explanations can sometimes be a means of convincing ourselves of something. Short, strong confirmatory yes or no can be empowering and insightful.

And there's more

How do leaders know they are authentic leaders? Do people tell them? They do what they say they will? Do *you* respond clearly on an issue that hasn't been managed totally satisfactorily in the organization, or do you soften the response in order not to hurt feelings?

Honesty means saying it *as it is*. You can be empathetic and sensitive when speaking to a colleague, but the delivery must not shirk away from the message to be delivered. It is also important to be sure the message has been received.

The questions below are not easy to answer. They will take some time especially if you ask the supplementary question, "So what do I do now?"

- ✓ In what ways do your actions speak louder than your words?
- ✓ What concrete evidence do you have to support your answer?
- ✓ Is there, within you, a genuine passion for, and belief in, what the organization stands for?
- ✓ What evidence could others provide to authenticate this?
- ✓ Would trust be a word colleagues would use?
- ✓ What would your colleagues say as they reflect on their working relationship with you?
- ✓ How do you work with colleagues who have similar talents and aspirations to your own?

Any surprises? No matter how diligently we follow actions outlined in previous chapters, our impact as a leader will be significantly reduced, if not derailed, if we are not viewed as trustworthy. If colleagues believe we do not operate with integrity, then our attempts to bring them confidently onside will be thwarted. Focus truthfully on the leadership style that you believe is yours and test it out. Keep *your* new checklist handy.

Leaders are always honest, aren't they?

This is a highly sensitive area and one that requires some significant soul-searching for aspiring and developing leaders. *Are* leaders honest at all times? We know this can't be the case by the law of averages, yet it should be what we at least aspire to be. However, there are leaders who demonstrate ruthless, combative, and aggressive behaviors as they claw their way to the top. These attributes can form the preferred leadership style of some.

Which of the two leadership behaviors are closest to you? Are you the aspirant leader or the ruthless leader? There may also be a sneaking admiration for the ruthless seemingly successful leader.

There can be an unspoken thought that the leader demonstrating care and integrity is weak. The model you are developing may have some of both. This is your first and perhaps most important question to answer: Which combination are you?

How can you earn trust?

Whichever the organization, large or small, colleagues' trust must be earned. It isn't handed over with the new job. Trust can only be established as a result of genuinely good actions and deeds. There are no shortcuts. Achieving trust depends on consistency of actions and a daily demonstration that says trust matters.

There isn't a magical tick list that will miraculously result in everyone trusting a leader. Consistency of behavior and transparency in decision-making needs to be evident. These will eventually be recognized as *authentic* actions if thoughtfully adhered to.

Leaders have values

Making personal values and beliefs in the workplace evident each day helps people understand the person a little better. They can see why a leader operates in a particular the way. Talking about them doesn't make them authentic. Simply telling people personal values and beliefs are important to you does not make colleagues believe it. What colleagues want to see demonstrated, and hear said, are a leader's beliefs and values in action. Authenticity must be worn with pride *and* humility.

Exploring

Is the office door always open to people because you tell people it is, or is it genuinely open? Saying so and fulfilling that promise is the commitment. If you have agreed to see someone at a specific date and time, then stick to it unless there are *very* good reasons. If a time change *must* be made, always reschedule then and there. People will appreciate that level of integrity and respect for both the individual whose time is being changed and the challenge that the leader faces.

The importance of team members knowing their concerns and views are of real importance and interest are data points a leader can use to track success. If this is not felt by team members, then the relationship remains broken and needs action to fix it. If every time someone passes the door and it is literally or metaphorically closed, then the first step to redemption is clear.

The discomfort of honesty

How many times have we witnessed public figures in the media saying *categorically* that they haven't done anything wrong when challenged by an investigation-based report? A few short weeks later, it becomes clear that they most certainly have. The person's credibility is gone, and often there is an aftershock from the public, who believed this person to be truthful and honest.

When a hero falls from grace, their demise is painful for all concerned. It will be equally painful if this happens to you. Don't pretend to be what you are not. Be proud of who and what you are and what you stand for. Your values are the essence of *you*, so let them be witnessed by others in your actions and deeds.

Maybe there are times when a leader finds themselves being excessively sharp or short-tempered. If this is regular behavior, and we are stressing the need to be true to yourself here, then you must stop and ask yourself, "Do I actually like this style? Do I like the results?"

If you don't like it, can you change, and what are those first steps?

Uncomfortable

If the answer is that while there is recognition as to how irritable you are with colleagues on occasions, this behavior brings the responses and actions that you want. If this is a yes, then you need to pull the emergency cord and stop.

This signifies the type of leader you are—impatient, disrespectful, and perhaps a bully. Do you like what you see?

We often hear people whose modus operandi is to be painfully blunt and frequently rude, excusing their behavior with the phrase, "What you see is what you get," or "I just say it as it is!"

It is as if this absolves them from the resultant fallout. It simply means a lack of care for the feelings of the person the leader is speaking to and little or no respect for them as an individual.

No excuses

Even if views are directly opposed to yours, it is important to show respect and listen. There is no excuse for rudeness. People who adopt this approach generally do so because this makes them feel powerful. Many mistake this approach as demonstrating strong leadership. This is similar in many ways to people who respond rudely and aggressively via social media. This isn't being honest or an effective leader. It is simply being at best rude and cowardly at worst.

William Benner, President of WW Consulting Inc, was previously an executive leadership adviser and consultant to the US Federal Reserve System. In a chapter headed *"Practicing Trustworthy Behaviors"* in a book entitled *Trust Inc.* by Barbara Brooks Kimmel, he states that "There is reduced confidence and declining expectations in governments, businesses, leadership, management, work teams, coworkers, and even friends on trust."

He writes, "Ask anyone to name five people they trust implicitly. They are hard-pressed to identify one or two, much less five individuals."

Name five

Would you be able to do that, and can you articulate *why?* We would all hope to feature in someone's "trust implicitly" list as we would like to think we exhibit the same tendencies as those we appreciate so much in others. Ah, if only that were true.

Staff should *never* see:

- ✓ One colleague receive four warnings before administrative action is taken
- ✓ One colleague receive only one warning and then be subject to administrative action
- ✓ Someone get away with it completely
- ✓ A leader issue a directive about the deadline and then does not carry it out.

Such inconsistency creates frustration and certainly does not build trust. It generates the view that the leader doesn't know what they are doing. Such behaviors are perceived as showing favoritism and lead to distrust in the workplace. Authentic leaders are consistent in their actions and demonstrate naturally their belief in fairness.

Leading with empathy

Supporting and growing a team's performance is where honesty and trust play two very important roles. These make the difference between genuine growth for the individual and the organization, or no growth as the team's output suffers as a result of neither being part of the organization's DNA. If the individual doesn't know they are underperforming and has no help in order to improve their work practice, then how can they hope to improve?

Good communication skills and a sincere, empathetic, and yet clear approach to the issues needing to be addressed helps both organizational and individual progress. The destructive element surfaces when a leader gossips about a colleague's underperformance, personal habits, or personal relationships. It is made worse when the leader is "charming itself" to the employee. This hypocrisy and gossip-focused leadership hurts everyone and creates a work environment that could become toxic. It lacks honest interactions amongst individuals. This approach is destructive and based on shaming colleagues. There is no quality leadership here.

A simple and clarifying example here. The words, "Oh, I think that decision about the work dress code that you made for your team was absolutely right." When shared later with another person becomes "Well, that decision on the new dress code is *so* unnecessary, and I think it is an awful decision which will affect the morale of the team."

Authentic leadership is clearly absent here. The ability to build trust is at best hampered and at worst destroyed. Colleagues *know* when you are being duplicitous, and a leader will very quickly lose both their respect and their trust. Colleagues will begin to behave anxiously and warily around the leader as they will not be sure what to do. How will they know that the decision made was made because the leader believed in it?

Real-life example

A colleague recounted a most startling occasion when they were in a very senior position working for many years within a perceived strong team that focused solely on ensuring children and students received the very best education possible. For years, colleagues traveled the globe, sharing this message and demonstrating a passion for and commitment to this core value. Colleagues in the small team were proud to belong to it as it was made up of committed, authentic leaders.

The shock came when Team A engaged Team B from a different part of the world. Team B's leader was combatively forthright, describing the team's beliefs in a way that was the polar opposite of Team A's beliefs and practices. Moments of surprise and not a little discomfort followed, then Team A colleagues began to courteously defend their position and beliefs, bringing examples from their experiences into the conversation and challenging perceived inaccuracies.

The conversation was in full swing when Team A members became aware of how silent one colleague was. The group was both perplexed and bemused all at once and felt a little let down. Their expectation was that their colleague would defend a belief that he had shared with countless schools over many years and which Team

A had worked with him on consistently over time. Team A members felt a mixture of shock but also of severe disappointment. They questioned the integrity of the work they had been doing with this colleague for years but also questioned why he hadn't spoken up. In the end, there was a reluctant acceptance that courage was lacking, and this colleague was viewed in a very different light. This altered the team's working relationship and eventually led to its breakup.

The smallest actions reap the *greatest* rewards.

Leaders need to know what they are doing, don't they?

Well, of course, they do! This sounds simple yet unfortunately cannot be guaranteed. A leader who knows what they are doing and sets about ensuring in a quiet and diligent way that the team does too builds confidence in a team. This leader is successful. Team members are quick to spot a leader who is out of their depth or past their sell-by date. Professional knowledge and being up to speed with organizational developments are the minimum requirements.

Poor leaders can adopt an arrogant, pompous manner and use a thin smoke screen to hide these deficiencies. They can keep a low profile, hoping that a team member will pick up a critical issue and run with it. Then most unacceptable but common practice occurs: blame a team member or team when the initiative is unsuccessful *or* take the full credit when praise is given.

A challenging situation can arise when a very skilled member of the team cannot bear to see the impact of the dysfunctional leader. They pull the others around them, and they work to survive. Team members know that their leader doesn't know how to resolve the issue and are just grateful that someone, *anyone*, is leading them forward.

Don't do that!

It is valuable to look at work set out by Bob and Gregg Vanourek, coauthors of *Triple Crown Leadership: Building Excellent, Ethical and*

Enduring Organizations[10] in which they describe some *"trust buster"* behaviors of leaders as follows:

1) Abusive behavior
2) Appreciation lacking
3) Accountability lacking
4) Arbitrary use of power
5) Blaming
6) Communication poor and secretive
7) Disloyalty
8) Favoritism
9) Micromanagement
10) Tolerating toxic behavior

This may seem a daunting list, and we may sadly have an example of each that comes from our experiences. We may wonder if it is possible at all to build a trustworthy team. The answer is, of course, yes, it is. It starts with a leader whose *values* are evident, who strives for *excellence*, who *values* the skills and input of the team. If someone has gained *your* trust, you will go that extra mile for them and they for you.

You can now build your own list of things you believe in:

- What do you value?
- What do you do well?
- What do you do, not quite as well as you would like?
- What don't you do?
- What do you aspire to be?

The creation of a virtual *bucket* may be very helpful. This is where the not-so-great behaviors can be placed and thrown away. Doing that makes a very big statement to you personally, about your intent to become a better leader.

---

[10] Bob Vanourek and Greg Vanourek, *Triple Crown Leadership: Building Excellent, Ethical, and Enduring Organizations* (McGraw Hill, 2012).

Are you the real deal?

Clear the path ahead. Remember that behaviors and actions need to be the real deal. They are not played out because you think they are the right thing to do. Your team will find you out and consider you a fake.

Focusing in on both the value and impact of trust and authenticity is worthwhile looking at the results of the [11] *Triscendance Trust Assessment of Leadership Teams.* The data was collected from a diverse group of organizations: academic, engineering, biomedical research, local government sectors, insurance, and pharmaceutical sectors and was focused on common themes regarding what trustworthy behaviors were deemed important by team members and leaders.

The highest-scoring statements around team behaviors when there is trust suggest that:

- Teams rally well and pull together when faced with a crisis.
- Team members and team leaders typically demonstrate integrity and sincerity with one another (authentic).
- Team members are perceived as having the necessary skills and expertise to accomplish the team's objectives.

The lowest-scoring statements when there is no apparent trust indicate:

- Difficulty in raising issues of individual trust and performance with team members
- Concern that not all information is shared in team conversations
- Team members do not typically have conversations with each other when they have concerns about one another.

---

[11] Triscendance Trust's Assessment of Leadership Teams (www.triscendance.com, 2008–2011).

What is both reassuring and yet alarming is that the issues we have been exploring about leadership and the actions of effective leaders are the *same* regardless of the industry or organization you work in. The importance of reflecting on how you and your team can improve is imperative if you are to build trust and inspire a team to be great. You want to be a leader of a team that believes the highest-scoring statements reflect how they and you work together as a collaborative group.

Information from sources such as the *Triscendance Trust's Assessment of Leadership* is often helpful in confirming concerns you may have. It also puts under microscope practices and behaviors that need to be changed. There is quite a difference in knowing internally what you believe the impact of a good or a bad leader will have on a team and having it confirmed in such a clear and evidence-rich way.

[12]In the book *Mistakes Were Made (but Not by Me): Why We Justify Foolish Beliefs, Bad Decisions and Hurtful Acts*, authors Carol Tavris and Elliott Aronson note, "In the final analysis, the test of a nation's character and an individual's integrity does not depend on being error free. It depends on what we do after making the error."

We are learning this together—a high octane and powerful message that digs deep into core values, inner beliefs, and personality. The journey has been lengthy so far, complex and very demanding. How we behave today makes a very big difference to tomorrow.

Power of 3

Three quotations:

> Authentic leaders have insight and exert influence. ("The Five Marks of Authentic Leadership," Michael Hyatt)

---

[12] Carol Tavris and Elliot Aronson, *Mistakes Were Made (But Not by Me): Why We Justify Foolish Beliefs, Bad Decisions, and Hurtful Acts* (Mariner Books, 2007).

Authentic leaders are courageous, speak from the heart, build teams and create communities. (Holden Leadership Center, https://holden.uoregon.edu/leadership)

The only way to make a man trustworthy is to trust him. (Henry L. Stimson, US politician [1867–1950])

Three books to challenge your thinking further:

- Pink, Daniel. *Drive.* Riverhead Books, 2012.
- Blanton, Brad. *Radical Honesty.* Sparrowhawk Publisher.
- MacKenzie, Mindy. *The Courage Solution.* Greenleaf Book Group Press, 2016.

CHAPTER 9

Confidently Showing the Real Me

Reading and researching leadership with all its many facets provides almost too much information to digest and consider. If not carefully curated, it can encourage leaders to implement too much artificial and rapid change and to fall into the trap of the latest trends. This can be particularly true of people new to leadership, intent on making their mark. Leaders being seen doing without thinking through the potential impact creates the wrong first impression.

Being true to yourself, your values, and beliefs is a powerful guide to what comes next and why. *Staying* true to yourself, having self-efficacy, is the challenge. As a new leader, either for the first time or with a new team, demonstrating your belief that you are bringing something different to the organization's table is important. The challenge is to be sure that having a positive impact on the team or the team's target is the driving force. It is very important that these decisions are not seen as putting the "*I*" into "team."

Demonstrating an understanding of the balance of what is already in place within the team before making changes is a skillful line to walk. A new leader may fear bringing something new to the team/organization as it may be rejected. Working to fit in at any cost is an error new leaders should not make. It creates an image of someone under-confident—someone hesitant to make and commit to a final decision, someone unclear about how to build a team.

You may feel now that there are almost too many leadership skills, strategies, and attitudes to reflect upon. You have had opportunities throughout to review, consider, and plan. Deciding where to go next should be based on your enhanced skills and your reflections. Next up is, fundamentally, a focus on "others" and how you will relate to and lead them. How you intend and manage to create the conditions for followership and trust. Exactly what *will* you do?

Here I am—what now?

You may feel like the lemming, standing at the edge of the cliff, hesitant, and yet knowing it is time to step off, leading others to an exciting future or leading them to an organizational or career death. As a new leader, it is the leap of faith into your new way of working. A feeling of exhilaration with a healthy mix of anxiety can lead to the transformational moment and the realization, "I *can* do this!"

Steve Jobs, during his time as CEO of Apple, is quoted as saying, "It doesn't make sense to hire smart people and tell them what to do. We hire smart people so they can tell us what to do."

In other words, *be* the change you want to happen.

Courageously unique

Marcus Buckingham and Curt Coffman in their book, *First, Break All the Rules*[13], report on work that the organization Gallup undertook in the late 1990s based on interviewing people who had been identified by their company as great managers. Gallup wanted to systematically compare their answers to set questions to those of moderately successful managers. They interviewed team leaders, sports coaches, hotel managers, public school superintendents, military personnel, and countless other owners of similar roles. What was

---

[13] Marcus Buckingham and Curt Coffman, *First, Break All the Rules: What the World's Greatest Managers Do Differently.* Audiobook reporting on work the organization Gallup had undertaken in the late 1990s. Publisher: Brilliance Audio (unabridged edition), August 23, 2016.

it that the best managers/leaders did that made them so successful? Why was what they did perceived as successful by their teams?

A complete surprise! This research found that they didn't have much in common at all! They had different ways to motivate, build relationships, and set direction. The *common* element was that the successful leaders recognized that each team member working for them is *unique*, and they used that knowledge to provide opportunities for individuals to grow toward attaining their specific potential. They did not work to ensure everyone had the same skill set or behave *in the same way*, following the same rules. Instead, these great leaders recognized that a team benefits from combined and collaborative *uniqueness* and did not fear that such individuality might create disharmony. Consider the examples below:

Real-life example

Alan Mulally, former CEO of the Ford Motor Company. Mulally is recognized globally as having saved the Ford Company and changing their fortunes by altering their risk-averse culture. He didn't resort to bailouts or bankruptcy; instead he challenged the workforce rigorously and determinedly to rise to the challenge of change. He streamlined teams to ensure the right people were in the right roles. Mulally brought his finely honed specific leadership skills and approach to a failing organization and challenged it confidently, courageously, and determinedly.

There were too many people who had been there for too long (simply put, they had to go in a rigorous restructure) and responsibilities and accountabilities had to be redefined with everyone clear as to what was expected from them. He was most likely unpopular in the beginning as he was radically changing working practices with belief and speed. In 2014, the company made $7.2 billion and paid out $8.8k profit share to each worker. Mulally's approach may have been much more popular at this point!

Be the lemming

Now it is time to get out there and do it. The checklist below may be helpful as you navigate this new leadership opportunity.

- Place well-being (your and others) as one of your core values.
- Encourage the team to feel confident in expressing opinions, showing their judgments are valued and can contribute to team success.
- Recognize and embrace the value of being part of a diverse, global workforce.
- Encourage the team to take risks and not fear mistakes.
- Empower the team to feel secure in their environment.
- Model care, courtesy, collaboration.

The fabulous four

This list above is not exhaustive by any means, and you may have already defined the strategies you want to use immediately. If challenged to choose *just four* to begin with, what would they be and why? Whatever these personal actions are, the aim of a leader is to work out, eventually knowing intuitively how to choose the right one at the right time for the right outcome. By operating honestly and with clarity, colleagues are being given the chance to decide whether they are with you or not. Everyone deserves to be allowed to make that choice. A great leader shows clearly what these choices are.

Real-life example

Wendy Kopp, Cofounder of "Teach for All," harnessed her passion for education reform based on her Princeton University senior thesis and recruited social entrepreneurs in thirty-two countries to become teachers in underfunded "public" schools. Her ability to engage and inspire others means that thousands of children are benefitting. She dared to determinedly follow her vision, and through opening herself up for others to see what made her tick, passionately driving her cause and convincing others to join her, she made a difference, narrowing educational disparities around the world.

Modeling, does it work?

Do great leaders model behaviors and values, and in what ways do they see this as an important element of communication? There are two distinct views about modeling. Some people believe that demonstrating how things should be done or how people should be treated is a basic requirement. It works because people can see by a leader's actions what is expected of them. Others believe that modeling or exemplifying only works if people observing want to see change and respond. Is modeling something you feel is important and will be used by you?

"Because you believed I was capable of behaving decently, I did" (Paulo Coelho, [14] *The Devil and Miss Prym*).

Becoming a servant leader

Being customer focused and wanting to be the most considerate and caring leader may be a strong motivator for you. You may believe that small things make a big difference. This may be where you model behaviors. Your style may be one of listening, celebrating success, and showing genuine appreciation of people's efforts. Your leadership style may be about building that sense of a team that puts customers, students, staff, and each other first.

Problem solver

Problem-solving is a form of thinking that is the most complex of all intellectual functions. It is a higher-order thinking skill. That may be the specific skill you want on your team to supplement your own skills or to close a gap.

---

[14] Paulo Coelho, *The Devil and Miss Prym* (HarperCollins Publisher, 2006).

The leader does not always have to be the problem solver. If you recognize that skill in others, empower them to use it. Exuding a sense of calmness in times of stress helps the team assess a situation and prevent perhaps previous mistakes, leading to improvement.

I want to be...

In the book [15]*Swimming with Sharks* by Joris Luyendijk, the author details an interview with a female ex-PR and communications director. She shared the fact that having spent ten years preventing people from spilling the beans on life inside the financial industry, she had quit. She recognized that when accompanying a senior leader during a press interview, she would halt or divert a question to retain the status quo. She did not allow the world to see what was happening, effectively blocking change. She was fully aware that the reality was being denied and opportunities to change the system thwarted.

Her comment was "Inside, I'd be screaming, 'Yes, that's exactly the question you *should* be asking!'"

That is not how you want to be feeling each day.

So...is the fog clearing?

Do you:

- Know what you want?
- Know what you need?
- Know how to get it?
- Know how the team thinks?
- Know what might be missing in the team?
- Feel you are beginning to know how you will lead?

William James, the American philosopher, says, "It is our attitude at the beginning of a difficult task which, more than anything else, will affect its successful outcome."

---

[15] Joris Luyendijk, *Swimming with Sharks* (Guardian Faber publishing, 2015).

Think things through now and don't rush. Take your time to *know*. Don't let your internal voice say, "You can't!" Let it lead you to the *how*. Know you *are* able. You *are* courageous! You *are* capable. You *are* proudly unique.

Unleashing others' potential

Now that you have some reflective strategies under your belt, you will recognize that you can't be good at everything. Encouraging colleagues to reflect after you, or the team, have completed a task ensures that a blame culture doesn't exist. This leadership style doesn't place blame on any one person; it helps everyone better understand what was successful and what could be better next time.

No blame here

The Red Arrows, the United Kingdom's Royal Air Force's aerobatic team, always review their performances whether in rehearsal or at an air show. They do not name each other when reviewing their performance. To emphasize the team-ness as key to the success of the team, they refer to their aircraft by number so that review and assessment may sound like this: "Red 1 too close to Red 3," "Red 2 timed the turn very well."

In this way, everyone learns and improves from review without anyone feeling embarrassed or undermined. Failure in this team would be catastrophic, and the smallest errors must be corrected. The message for you to take away from here: *always* find time to stop and reflect.

Your next big question

Moving from *me* to us. Be the leader who unleashes the potential of the team.

In your new or enhanced leadership role, are you now able to analyze the strengths and skill set of your colleagues? You will need people who are:

- *Organized* and able to deliver to deadlines
- *Creative*, practically or imaginatively, and who contribute in taking the organization to the next level
- *Disciplined* and contribute productively in all areas of their work
- *Collaborative* with colleagues who show consistently, maybe daily, how they value working alongside colleagues
- *Service-orientated*, the customer in whatever organization comes first regardless of which team member is dealing with them
- *Goal orientated* because you want the team, and themselves, to succeed
- *Competitive* in a collaborative way so that the team and not just the individual succeeds
- *Achieving* results due to the approach, knowledge, and commitment to the team goals
- *Values driven* as seen by their courteous, caring, and consistent approach to colleagues
- *Able to put thoughts directly into action*—that means colleagues who confidently get on with what they have to do with limited guidance and the constant need for reassurance
- *Problem solvers*, people in your team who are totally solution focused.

Lead your team. Be open, honest, and reflective. You *can* do it!

> *Start your plan!*
> *It's impossible, said Pride.*
> *It's risky, said Experience.*
> *It's pointless, said Reason.*
> *Give it a try, whispered the Heart!*
> (Attribution unknown)

ABOUT THE AUTHOR

Ann McPhee and Pam Mundy are experienced international leaders having operated in a range of environments such as education and business. Their work spans both strategic and operational roles in many international schools and organizations in many different countries. Their experiences range from leading international schools to serving on educational boards, often providing leadership support, guidance, and training to leaders and aspiring leaders at all levels. Coaching and mentoring are key elements of their work. A focus on building leadership strengths within business and school communities aims to enable sustainable growth in organizations, building capacity and skills. Ann and Pam have worked with investors and schools that have been newly acquired by larger companies, supporting a smooth transition demonstrating respect for the newly acquired organizations' achievements and its culture. Assignments have been in the US, Middle East, Latin America, South America, Russia, Southeast Asia, Europe, and the UK, with not-for-profit schools, for-profit schools, and charitable trusts. These experiences have expanded both mindsets and skill sets, proving that anything is possible provided there is a willingness to learn and have an openness to embracing unfamiliar environments and an ability to be adaptable. A passion for leading with respect enables their work to be successful.

Printed in the USA
CPSIA information can be obtained
at www.ICGtesting.com
LVHW042326140924
790864LV00001B/142